Growing Up With Clemente

Growing Up
With
Clemente

Richard Peterson

The Kent State University Press
Kent, Ohio

© 2009 by The Kent State University Press, Kent, Ohio 44242
ALL RIGHTS RESERVED.
Library of Congress Catalog Card Number 2008040102

ISBN 978-0-87338-982-2

Manufactured in the United States of America

Library of Congress Cataloging-in-Publication Data

Peterson, Richard F.
Growing up with Clemente / by Richard Peterson.
p. cm.

ISBN 978-0-87338-982-2 (pbk. : alk. paper) ∞

1. Clemente, Roberto, 1934–1972.   2. Baseball players—Puerto Rico—Biography.
3. Pittsburgh Pirates (Baseball team)—History.   4. Peterson, Richard F. I. Title.
GV865.C45P48 2009
796.357092—dc22
[B]
2008040102

British Library Cataloging-in-Publication data are available.

13 12 11 10 09   5 4 3 2 1

For Anita:
side by side

A 1951 Clyde Hare photograph of bridges looking up the Monongahela (courtesy of the Carnegie Library of Pittsburgh)

Chapter 1

Looking down from the observation deck on Mount Washington, visitors to Pittsburgh are often amazed at the beauty of my hometown.

In the clear sunlight, the spray from the fountain at Point State Park soars like the city's renaissance spirit. In the background, skyscrapers, standing in tribute to Pittsburgh's legendary industrial giants and the incredible wealth made from the bowels and hearths of western Pennsylvania, form a Golden Triangle at the confluence of the Allegheny and Monongahela rivers. At night, the lights from the scene below sparkle like a rich diamond field. The glowing rivers, once avenues of commerce for the coal and iron ore needed for Pittsburgh's fiery steel mills, flow by like molten streams of gold.

A century ago, visitors to Pittsburgh saw an entirely different city. So much soot and smoke billowed from its mills that English novelist Anthony Trollope, on a tour of America, called Pittsburgh "the blackest place . . . I ever saw." At night the fires from blast furnaces lit up the skies so dramatically that historian James Parton described the city as "hell with the lid taken off." H. L. Mencken saw a Pittsburgh landscape "so dreadfully hideous, so intolerably bleak and forlorn that it reduced the whole aspirations of man to a macabre and depressing joke."

I grew up in Pittsburgh in the late 1940s and 1950s. It was a time when clouds of smoke still darkened the city's skies, and industrial slime and human waste turned its rivers into a poisonous bile. World War II may have saved the city from the Great Depression, but the economic recovery also increased the pollution that had been strangling the city for generations. The smoke and soot were so bad by the end of the war that local politicians, industrialists, and financiers finally recognized that Pittsburgh had become a dying city.

The Greek philosopher Heraclitus once observed that the river we place our foot in today is not the river we placed our foot in yesterday, that the river's current, like time itself, is relentless and irreversible. But, from Mount Washington's observation deck, I can look up the Monongahela in the direction of Pittsburgh's South Side, where I grew up, and easily reverse the river's flow. In my mind's eye, I can move its current back in time, until I envision myself as a young teen, moving, with my working-class buddies, through the washed-up debris, discarded junk, and the empty bottles of cheap wine scattered along the bank of the Monongahela near the doomed Brady Street Bridge.

I can see the clearing where, on a hot summer day, we'd strip out of clothes ringed with sweaty grime, pull on our bathing suits, and head for the river's edge. In the same waters, where families now launch themselves out in recreation boats and a current generation of Pittsburgh's boys and girls of summer roar by on their Jet Skis, we'd wade out from shore on a deep layer of industrial sludge and move hundreds of yards through the swirling river before its murky water would rise to our chests. If a towboat appeared, we'd twist our feet ankle deep into the greasy gunk to see if the waves from its coal barges could dislodge us. When we began to swim, we'd have to keep our mouths closed so we wouldn't swallow the yellowed streaks of slime and the colorless nuggets of waste moving through the river's current.

As a young girl, my mother watched her brother Charlie become ill and die after he swam in the Monongahela on a hot Fourth of July. She hated the river, never learned to swim, and made me promise to keep my distance from its poisonous waters. But I loved the river and couldn't resist its lure no matter how many times I'd hear the story of Charlie. On hot summer days when I wanted to go swimming, I'd roll up my bathing suit inside a towel and tell my mother I was headed to the public pool at Ormsby playground. Afterward, I'd have to shower at Ormsby before I went back home because the chemical reek from my body and the black streaks on my legs were a dead giveaway that I'd broken my promise to stay away from the river.

The river was a summons to my youth. The Monongahela may have been waiting to fill my lungs with poison, if its sinkholes and whirlpools didn't drown me first, but, if I were willing to take the risk, the river had the mythic power to conjure up a world of extraordinary wonders and adventures lurking all around me. All I had to do was look up at the badly rusted and discolored Brady Street Bridge and my imagination would transform it into a steel colossus, a Joe Magarac, standing bestride my South Side, with its ethnic enclaves, and the Hill District, home to the city's largest black population. The river may have been a natural barrier between Pittsburgh's white and black worlds, but, if I had the strength and the courage, I could swim crosscurrent to the opposite shore and emerge into a storied and forbidden world, where numbers racketeers owned nightclubs and Negro League baseball teams, gamblers, with their pocket switchblades, played poker and shot craps at darkened speakeasies, and exotic women of the night strolled the streets and offered sex for money.

Unlike my mother, I'd learned how to swim, but the river's expanse was so daunting that I hadn't the heart or the strength to make it to the other side. I had to be content to float along in a warm current that, if I let it, would move me downriver under the Tenth Street Bridge, with its massive extension cables, then under the Smithfield Street Bridge leading into Downtown Pittsburgh, until, like a South Side Odysseus, I'd wash up on the shore of Point Park. But, after floating downriver for a few hundred yards, I'd grow nervous, hurriedly paddle back upriver, and, not yet ready for adventures beyond the South Side, return to shore and the working-class world of my childhood.

Several years later, as my teenage years and the decade of the 1950s were coming to an end, the Monongahela had lost its magic. I walked or rode over the Brady Street Bridge but rarely looked down at the river on my way out to Forbes Field, Pitt Stadium, or the Duquesne Gardens to watch a sporting event. The Hill District was now nothing more to me than a black slum, where, on occasion, I was forced to play on one of its rundown ball fields in a park district tournament game. Pittsburgh's Downtown, where my mother and I had gone on holiday weekends to visit department stores and watch matinee movies and stage shows, was now where I spent my dreary weekdays working as a stock boy.

But the river had one more surprise and mystery for me before I completely surrendered to adulthood. After spending a warm summer day moving stock around in the catacombs of Gimbels department store, I decided to walk home from Downtown instead of taking a claustrophobic streetcar or a bus back to the South Side. There was nothing eventful about the day at work or the walk home until I turned from Second Avenue and headed over the Tenth Street Bridge. Halfway over the bridge, I noticed a small boat circling in the river below as two men dragged thick lines in the water. A few minutes after I went over to the railing, I watched the men pull the body of a young man about my age to the river's surface.

I knew drownings were common enough in Pittsburgh's rivers, and that, with all the bridges, there would always be jumpers. They even leaped from bridges like the ones at Mission Street on the South Side and at Panther Hollow in Schenley Park that weren't over water. I also knew about men and boys, like my uncle Charlie, who hadn't jumped but still died because of the river, about the B-25 bomber crew that crashed upriver and was never found, and about the deck men from riverboats who fell into the river and were swept under by its currents.

But I was shocked at seeing the dark, matted hair and the pale, bloated face suddenly appear out of the water. Looking down from the railing as the men pulled the soaking, dripping body into the boat, I imagined the horror of swimming in the river and bumping into a corpse floating just beneath the water. I also remembered what it was like to be submerged in water so murky you couldn't see your hand in front of your face, and I wondered if the young man, after plunging into the river, had panicked and struggled against the river's green cloud before his lungs filled with the poisonous water.

I watched the boat head downriver, where the body would be taken to the city morgue and, if it had no identification, placed on display behind glass panels for curiosity seekers or worried families looking for a lost son. Looking after the boat, I wondered if the jumper had grown up on the South Side. Maybe he felt suffocated by the pungent odor from the Duquesne brewery and the black soot from the Jones and Laughlin steel mill or trapped by the South Side's insulated, parochial world of neighborhood stoops, church pews, and bar stools. Perhaps he worried that he'd spend his adult life buried in a community resistant and even hostile to change, because our fathers and mothers had taught us from their own hard experiences that life on the South Side, if it changed at all, usually did so for the worse.

As I walked down the bridge's incline to the South Side, I thought about my own life and wondered if, in the flow of my own childhood memories, I might find the answer to the mystery of the drowned young man. More than that, I wanted to know whether it was my youthful joy as I floated in the river and imagined a world of wonders or a young man's despair as he stood on the bridge and stared down at the only escape imaginable from an unbearable existence that was the true reflection of growing up on Pittsburgh's South Side.

I was haunted for a long time by the image of the drowned young man, but the answer to my own fate was not lurking in the river's dark current. The river may have been a siren's call to my youth, but playing ball on Pittsburgh's playgrounds and journeying out to Forbes Field to watch the Pirates had also fired my imagination. I also had no way of knowing that within a year after the disturbing incident on the bridge, the Pittsburgh Pirates, led by the great Roberto Clemente, would lift my spirit as well as the spirit of the entire city by winning a dramatic World Series and setting the stage for my decision to seek a life beyond the river and the South Side's steel mills and beer joints.

When I was growing up on the South Side, the current of my working-class life was as strong and treacherous as the river's, but the simple pleasures of playing catch in the alley with my father, walking around the corner to Ormsby playground for a pickup game, hitch-hiking out to Forbes Field to see the Pirates, and dreaming of playing in the big leagues would often lift me through the dangers. Out of the flood of memories that I have of the hard life on the South Side, the most important flow from Pittsburgh's ball fields.

Chapter 2

I was born in Pittsburgh in April 1939, less than five months before Hitler began World War II by invading Poland. I entered first grade in September 1945, a month after the war was over. My schoolmates and I were the war-babies generation, the pre–baby boomers, who would grow up struggling to find an identity in a postwar era of anxieties and alienation. We were the confused and sometimes lost souls from a generation that no historian would call the greatest, a generation that never did find a cause, and that would eventually find itself usurped and converted by television nostalgia into the merry band of teenagers on *Happy Days*. Only the mediocrity of television, the defining cultural force of our time, could transform James Dean's character in *Rebel without a Cause* into the Fonz.

Growing up on the working-class South Side, we were also the sons and daughters of fathers who, when they weren't fighting and winning a war, spent their days in steel mills, gas stations, and warehouses and their nights in neighborhood beer joints. Our working mothers wanted to stay home but ended up as waitresses, sales clerks, and cleaning women just to make ends meet. Our parents, children of the late-nineteenth and early-twentieth century wave of Eastern European immigrants, were the first generation to speak without a foreign accent, the first to attend American schools, though they dropped out early to find work, and the first to hide their ethnicity by Anglicizing their last names. In my father's family, the Lithuanian "Petrauskas," translated as "son of Peter," became "Peterson" for my father and his brothers.

Those of us who started first grade at Humboldt grade school in 1945 were mostly the mutts and runts of the South Side's working class and

Second grade class at Humboldt, 1946. Peterson second from right, second row.

its ethnic enclaves. We were the children who went to public school instead of one of the South Side's Catholic schools. While priest-fearing Catholic families who could afford it proudly dressed their daughters in skirted uniforms and their sons in white shirts and black ties and sent them off to Lithuanian St. Casimir's, Polish St. Adalbert's, or German St. Michael's to be taught their catechism by yardstick-wielding nuns, we slouched our way in jerseys and dungarees toward Humboldt to read about WASPish Dick and Jane and their dog Spot. Having muddled our way through six years of a hardscrabble life on the South Side, we were now in the hands of a coterie of female public schoolteachers, most of them with "Miss" in front of their last names, and all determined to drill and paddle an education into the unfit.

Humboldt, an aging two-story, late-Victorian building, had been one of the first public schools constructed in Pittsburgh, its history dating back to 1867. It was located just a handful of city blocks from my home and was an easy ten-minute walk to school each morning. It was close enough that I could hurry back home at lunchtime for a hastily made jumbo or chipped ham sandwich and a bottle of pop before reluctantly heading back to Humboldt until the three o'clock bell sent me scurrying back home again.

Because Humboldt was located only three blocks from St. Casimir's, I was also part of an odd cross-migration of Casimir and Humboldt

7

My father, Frank Peterson, in his gas station uniform, circa 1945.

kids on every school day. My schoolmates and I, as we crossed paths with our Catholic counterparts, had to wait until sixth-grade patrol boys with their white safety belts waved us across the busy South Side streets. Once we reached Carson Street, the South Side's main drag, we waited again until Mrs. O'Hara, in her skirted police uniform, held up her gloved hand to stop traffic, blew her whistle, and waved us across the last dangerous intersection on our way to Humboldt. St. Casimir kids were on their own, but they did have their St. Christopher medals to guide them through the heavy traffic and the knowledge that, if they were run over, their souls were bound for heaven.

I went to Humboldt instead of St. Casimir's, but, the offspring of a mixed marriage, I could have gone to a public or private school. My father, Frank, was the Catholic son of Lithuanian parents who could barely speak English. A teenager during the Great Depression, he dropped out of school early and found work in gas stations around the South Side. An unhappy, intelligent man, he tried to drink away his inner demons, only to become more miserable as he drank. After a day of fixing flats, greasing cars, and pumping gas, he'd walk around the corner after supper to Kalki's for a familiar barstool and evening drafts of beer, with an occasional boilermaker mixed in if he had the money or if the bartender was in a generous mood. By the time my mother was ready to leave for her graveyard shift as a waitress and counter girl at Rodger's in Pittsburgh's Oakland district, he'd be back home, seated at the kitchen table with a bottle of Iron City or Fort Pitt. After my mother headed out the door to catch the 77/54 streetcar for her twenty-minute ride to work, he was ready to announce, almost tauntingly, to my younger sister Nancy and me, that "goin' to sleep was the best part of the day." His drinking cost him jobs, but at least his high blood pressure kept him out of the war.

My mother, Lillian, the Protestant daughter of English parents from the slums of Liverpool, had to be a surrogate wife to her father, along with her two sisters, Alice and Bert, after their mother died when they were barely in their teens. Her marriage was to have been her escape from a tyrannical father who routinely showed his displeasure at supper by flipping over his plate and waiting for his daughters to prepare something more fitting for a day laborer at the South Side Hospital. My grandfather Whitehouse liked to feed his English Collie with scraps

My mother, Lillian Peterson, in waitress uniform, circa 1950.

from the table, but occasionally he'd dip a fried potato in vinegar just to watch Queenie bite into it, then yelp out at the bitterness of the taste. My mother didn't know about my father's heavy drinking until after she married him, but her mean-spirited father had certainly prepared her for the hard life.

I don't know why Nancy and I were baptized Protestants instead of Catholics, but I always assumed it had something to do with getting my

English grandfather to approve, however reluctantly, of my mother's marriage to a "heathen Catholic." But, even if we had been baptized Catholics, I doubt if we would have gone to St. Casimir's because it seemed like we were always hurting for money. My family, except for my mother's abortive attempt at a Christmas Club, never had a bank account, never had any savings, and never owned a house. We did briefly own a car, but my mother made my father get rid of it when she found him passed out in the front seat after a night of heavy drinking. The next morning she told him, that with all the beer joints on the South Side, he didn't need "no goddamn car to get drunk."

When I started first grade at Humboldt, my family was living with my father's Lithuanian parents in an old, two-story wooden house on Merriman Way, a South Side back alley near the polluted Monongahela River. My grandparents and, for a time, my uncle Tony and his new wife Nellie, occupied the three rooms on the first floor, while we lived in two of the three rooms upstairs. With only a kitchen stove and a small electric heater in the bedroom to keep us warm, we used the third room—we called it the "cold room"—for storage in the summer and as an icebox in the winter. With no upstairs toilet, my father and I peed in the sink and my mother used a bedpan. If I had to do something more than pee, I took some newspaper, but not from the comics or the sports section, to the downstairs toilet in the small, unheated closet next to my grandparents' bedroom. Since there was no shower or bathtub, I had to endure an occasional scrubbing at the sink from my mother or, worse yet, a dunking in a corrugated washtub. But it wasn't bad afterward, bundled up in a blanket, sitting Indian-style on top of the heated oven, sipping a hot cup of angel's tea with milk and sugar, and listening intently to "The Shadow," "Inner Sanctum," and "Gang Busters" on the small, family radio perched on the kitchen mantel.

As far back as I can remember, my grandfather "Ignas," or Ignatius, made his living, or at least made enough to buy food and coal, by collecting junk and selling it to the corner scrap yard. In the mornings he roamed the neighborhood with his empty wheelbarrow, looking through neglected yards and abandoned lots, picking through the leavings behind the alley's rag factory, and inspecting the debris around Levinson Steel and the Iron City Sand and Gravel Company. By late afternoon, like a Lithuanian Ben Franklin, he pushed his wheelbarrow,

My Petrauskas
grandparents,
circa 1950.

now loaded with junk, up over the alley's uneven red bricks and tar patches into our backyard, where he sorted everything into small piles for selling or saving in his sheds. He distrusted the handful of black families on the block and his nosy grandson, and kept his sheds locked when he was out scavenging.

While my grandfather had the gaunt, angular figure and unpleasant scowl of an unhappy wanderer in search of anything but a job, my grandmother "Kotryna," or Katherine, had the wide and happy appearance—with her rosy cheeks, white-haired bun, and perpetual apron—of a woman who lived for holy days of obligation, carefully circled on her religious calendar, and for the early Sunday Mass celebrated in Lithuanian at St. Casimir's. As if to compensate for her husband's junk piles and brooding silences, she kept a small vegetable garden in the backyard, where she grew her *kopustai, agurkai,* and *pomidorai,* and a chicken coop, where my Easter peeps grew out of their coloring and disappeared into my grandmother's oven. Every morning she urged me to be a "good boy for teacher" as I headed up to Humboldt, and every afternoon she scolded me for bringing home "no books, no good" from school. But that never stopped her from inviting me into her kitchen for a cup of bitter "kava" and sweet "sokoladas" and a gentle plea to "no tell mama, I spoil supper."

In working-class families with strong ethnic traditions, Christmas, after a hard year of struggle and sacrifice, was usually celebrated as a day of plenty. In our family, Christmas supper in my grandparents' downstairs kitchen was always the high and low point of the holiday. I remember looking forward, after spending a cold day in our drafty, poorly heated upstairs rooms, to the nearly stifling heat from my grandfather's coal-burning pot-bellied stove and the strong, seductive odors of my grandmother's cooking. Christmas supper, prepared by my grandmother Petrauskas, was an array of delights and horrors from the old country. Besides the traditional ham and richly buttered mashed potatoes, my favorites were the *balandeliai,* wrapped in cabbage leaves and cooked in tomato sauce, and the *kugelis,* with its rich taste of bacon and potatoes.

My grandmother always wanted me to try everything, but I just couldn't stomach my father's foul-smelling favorites, like the marinated herring and the jellied pig's feet, and I was not going to put horseradish on my ham no matter how many times my father claimed it was "gonna put some hair" on my anemic-looking chest. It was enough that I had to take one of the tasteless waferlike *plotkele* blessed by Father Walter at St. Casimir's midnight mass and, after an approving nod from my Protestant mother, had to chew and swallow it as my grandmother hugged and wished everyone *Su Sventom Kaledom.*

But my most enduring memories of Christmas supper with my grandparents never end happily or merrily, despite my grandmother's Christmas blessing. After her toast something always goes wrong. My father, after drinking all day, either starts in about my picky eating—I should be eating with my "Johnny Bull" relatives instead of with the Petrauskas "Bluetails"—or about my mother's waitress job at Rodger's— she's "gone all goddam night and sleeps all goddam day"—or about my mother's fooling around with customers—he'd like to know "where the money for presents came from, if we're so goddam broke." It's time he got "some goddam respect" from his family. Once he's working again— "things are gonna be different, just yunz wait and see." By the end of the meal, my grandfather has walked away from the kitchen table in disgust and taken the bottle of Seagram's with him, my grandmother is telling her son, "for shame, Frankie" for ruining supper, and my mother is telling me to go with my father so he "don't break his goddam neck" staggering back upstairs.

My grandmother fretted about my education once I left for Humboldt each weekday morning, but she had nothing to worry about when it came to the three Rs. At Humboldt, I was taught to read those innocuous sentences about Dick and Jane and their idyllic middle-class lives. It was where I spent endless hours practicing my cursive writing according to the Palmer method and learned my arithmetic tables by rote. I also had to memorize "I think that I shall never see / A poem as lovely as a tree," though the only trees growing on the South Side's dumps and lots were the foul-smelling trees of heaven. In my school tablet with the map of Pennsylvania on the cover, I tried to get the words from Joyce Kilmer's sappy poem out of my head by drawing picture after picture of dogfights between P-51 Mustangs and German Messerschmitts or P-40 Flying Tigers and Jap Zeroes, while dreaming of becoming a fighter pilot in the off-season when I wasn't playing for the Pittsburgh Pirates.

I read in the *Weekly Reader* that the world beyond the South Side was a dangerous place, darkened by the threat of mushroom clouds, divided by an Iron Curtain, and infiltrated by Russian spies. After reading an underwater adventure story in my *Reader,* I briefly contemplated becoming a deep-sea diver, though playing baseball for the Pirates, even to my preadolescent mind, seemed more realistic than shooting down the Russian Migs that were replacing the Jap Zeros of my war-hero fantasies or finding tiger sharks or a giant squid instead of the three-headed catfish rumored to be swimming in the toxic Monongahela.

I may have been a working-class mutt, but I was also street-smart enough to be a straight-S student at Humboldt without much of an effort. I even appeared on Pittsburgh's version of the popular Whiz Kids radio show and, after missing my first question because I didn't know flax from cotton, helped Humboldt defeat a rival public school and won a fountain pen. I waited and sweated at the microphone, praying for a question on war or baseball, but when I was asked who saved Captain John Smith, I paused, waited for my head to clear and my heart to stop pounding, and nervously whispered, "Pocahontas?"

In my years at Humboldt, which began at the end of the Second World War and ended at the beginning of the Korean War, my education in the three Rs was supplemented by Miss Lamb's music class, where we learned to sing in harmony and dance the polka, though Miss Lamb always made sure that boys whirled around the room with boys, and girls with girls. Miss Lamb also directed Humboldt's occasional and feeble attempts at a school play. In my one memorable moment in the spotlight, I played a cowardly Little Jack Horner who was chased off the stage by a spider after smugly declaring "what a good boy am I" and vowing to protect the fair Miss Muffet. I was also selected by Miss Lamb to sing a solo number at a holiday program at one of the local radio stations. But, after my harrowing experience as a Whiz Kid, I faked an illness, fully intending to stay home from school until my voice changed. I still had my high tenor voice when my mother eventually forced me back to school, but the strategy worked because by then Miss Lamb had a new soloist for the program.

While Miss Lamb, who resembled Kate Smith in girth and loved hugging her kids, tried to lift our working-class spirits in song and dance, Miss Healy, our gym teacher, pursued the principle of a sound mind in a sound body with a vengeance. Humboldt's gym was a torture chamber of smelly mats, Indian clubs, vaulting horses, chin bars, and thick, coarse ropes dangling from the ceiling. It was where physically unfit children, accustomed to filling our lungs with the South Side's brewery-tainted, soot-filled air, tried desperately to keep up with Miss Healy as we performed bone-jarring jumping jacks to help with our coordination, then ran knee-jerking lap after lap around the gym to help with our endurance. Occasionally, to create a spirit of competition, Miss Healy started up a game of dodge ball, where bullies took out their anger on the bodies and heads of tearful girls, then turned their working-class rage on puny and uncoordinated boys.

It was in Humboldt's schoolyard, however, rather than in the classroom and the gym, that our real education, at least for the boys, took place. At recess the daughters of Rosie the Riveter took post-war refuge in games of hop scotch and jump rope, then went home to play with dolls and cut-outs and prepare for the domestic life, though there wasn't much chance they'd live happily ever after in some Pittsburgh version of Levittown. The war-lusting sons of returning service men ran wild at games of base and tag, then went home to toy tanks, planes, and ships to kill off more "Japs" and Nazis and dream of another world war, though all we would get in the 1950s was something called a "police action" against the "Gooks."

It was also in the schoolyard where boys were introduced prematurely to sex by leering at the dirty pictures on playing cards or the dirty drawings in blue-covered pocket comic books stolen from the stash of someone's uncle or father. In those anatomically exaggerated comic books, we learned the real reason Straight Arrow was called Straight Arrow and Joe Palooka was classified as a heavyweight. We also discovered to our astonishment and admiration why Olive Oyl squealed every time Popeye ate his spinach and why Daisy Mae, and every other female in Dog Patch, madly pursued Lil' Abner on Sadie Hawkins Day. At the end of recess we'd let the girls get in line ahead of us, so we could bump into them on our way back to class. They thought we were being rude and silly, but we were just trying to feel for something still beyond our grasp, at least until our hormones exploded in junior high.

Another major part of my education, beyond Humboldt's classrooms and schoolyard, went on in the dark at the Arcade, Colonial, Rex, and Liberty, the four movie houses on the South Side. Every Friday night of my early boy's life, while my father spent the lion's share of his working-class pay in one of his favorite beer joints, my mother and I spent four-bits to escape the hard life in the smoke-filled darkness of a movie theatre. I loved all of it, the romantic adventures, the musical comedies, the biblical epics, but my favorites were those Hollywood war movies, filled with patriotism and propaganda, in which brave Americans fought on remote islands to the bitter end, then returned, like General MacArthur, to finish off the Japs once and for all. I was so gullible and taken by war movies that, after watching *Thirty Seconds Over Tokyo*, I really did believe Van Johnson when he told his screen wife not to be upset about the leg he lost in the Doolittle raid because he'd just grow it back. He may have been kidding to comfort his wife, but I took great comfort in knowing that if I lost an arm or a leg shooting down Tokyo Joe, the villain of *God Is My Co-Pilot,* my favorite war movie, that, lizardlike, I'd just grow the limb back.

The movies were turning me into a war lover, but they were also feeding my budding love affair with baseball. A game of catch with my father was fun, but watching Hollywood turn baseball into the stuff of dreams was even better. The movies gave me everything from inspirational biographies to wacky comedies. I watched a tragic Lou Gehrig and a misunderstood Babe Ruth hit home runs to inspire sick and crippled kids and hummed along as a double-play combination, played by Frank Sinatra and Gene Kelly, who grew up in Pittsburgh dreaming about playing shortstop for the Pirates, sang and danced their way through "Take Me Out to the Ball Game." I also marveled at a wood-repellent liquid that made a baseball hop magically over a baseball bat in *It Happens Every Spring.*

I loved all those sappy, silly baseball movies, but my favorite was *The Stratton Story.* I seemed to have an early fixation on one-legged Hollywood heroes because *The Stratton Story* was about a big-league pitcher, played by Jimmy Stewart, who loses part of his right leg in a hunting accident. With the help of his devoted wife, played by June Allyson, and an equally supportive artificial leg, Stratton comes back to win a game against a team of all-stars as a voice in the background intones, "He stands as an inspiration to all of us, as living proof of what a man can do if he has the courage and determination to refuse to admit defeat." As much as I needed heroes, I also had my eye on girl-next-door June Allyson, who along with tomboy Betty Hutton and the athletic Esther Williams were the inspiration for my prepubescent daydreams. Apparently the girl that I marry "would have to be / as soft and as sweet as a nursery" but also capable of playing a good game of catch and swimming the English Channel.

My mother and I would usually go to the spacious and respectable Arcade on Twentieth and Carson because it showed double features direct from their first run at Downtown movie houses. The Arcade also had a Friday night jackpot drawing where you could win anything from fifty-cents to five dollars. It wasn't as palatial as Downtown movie houses like the Warner, Stanley, or Loew's Penn, but the Arcade was the only movie house on the South Side with a balcony. You had to be with an adult to get past the velvet rope that separated unfit kids from the best movie seats on the South Side, but, later on, when I was old enough to go to the Arcade with my buddies, we'd sneak past the usher, dive under the rope, and dash up the stairs because a front-row balcony seat was the perfect launching pad for pieces of hard-candied Boston Baked Beans, at least until the usher spotted us with his flashlight and kicked us back downstairs.

The Colonial, Rex, and Liberty, with their gutter urinals, smelly seats, and sticky floors, were the ugly stepsisters of the Arcade, but they did offer a steady stream of black-and-white B movies from the 1930s and 1940s. The Colonial was where Bogart and Cagney taught me that crime didn't pay, though I loved the gunplay and learned the proper way to take a bullet in the gut. It was also where I watched all those monster movies and their endless sequels featuring the Frankenstein monster, Count Dracula, the Wolfman, and an incredible Mummy, who couldn't use one arm, dragged one leg, yet, to my horror-stricken delight, still caught his terrified victims by the throat and strangled them. When I needed a break from movie monsters, I also had those hour-long "oaters" at the Liberty where Gene Autry, Roy Rogers, and Rocky Lane, billed as "the last of the singing cowboys," kept the West safe, in between yodels, from crooked sheriffs, marauding cattle rustlers, and rampaging Redskins.

I loved going to the Arcade with my mother on Friday night, but nothing topped going to the Rex on Saturday afternoon with my cousins to watch the latest chapter from some serial or cliffhanger. My mother and I would walk down to 17th Street where her married sisters, Alice and Bert, still lived with and took care of my grandfather. Before the sisters went shopping together, they bought us a bag of oranges from Goldberg's fruit market, just next door to the Rex, where, after they paid for our tickets, we peeled and munched away as characters from the comics and the radio came to life, only to die each week in some fiery crash or explosion, when they weren't being crushed to death by collapsing walls.

We watched Batman and Robin save Gotham City from a Nazi death-ray machine, and rode to the rescue with Zorro and other masked heroes like Don Daredevil and the female Black Whip. The chapters even had sex on display if you were willing to follow Nyoka the Jungle Girl or the White Goddess into peril after peril. They looked great in tight shorts and ripped blouses as they fled from jungle beasts and beastly villains, but no Jungle Girl or White Goddess could compete with the sight of the big-breasted Panther Girl, whose writhing struggle in quicksand was enough to stop us in mid-munch. We watched the ubiquitous Buster Crabbe play super-heroes ranging from Flash Gordon to Thunda, the King of the Congo, but we needed all the heroes we could get because evil Roy Barcroft, the master villain of the chapters, was always lurking about, ready, as the Martian Purple Monster or Retik the Ruler of the Moon, to invade and enslave the earth, even as we sat there.

When the chapter was over, we prepared to do battle with each other by crawling under our seats with bags of orange peels as unsuspecting moviegoers, after surviving another cliffhanger ending, settled back in their seats to watch a matinee double bill usually of old war movies. The war was over, but we were still learning from the movies that the merciless Japs had machine-gunned our pilots as they dangled helplessly from parachutes, used their bayonets on our wounded and defenseless soldiers, and then booby-trapped their dead bodies. But the biggest danger for moviegoers at the Rex was being caught in the crossfire when two kids suddenly rose between the aisles and started throwing orange peels at each other to competing shouts of "take that Tojo."

When I wasn't attending grade school or watching movies, I was completing my pre-pubescent education in the South Side's alleys, lots, and fields. Among the white kids living on Merriman Way were the brothers Jethro and Jerome, hillbilly transplants from West Virginia, and the alley's bully, dimwitted Joey Chisel, who had trouble saying his Rs—Pirate pitcher Bill Werle became "Burr Wurr"—and once got his arm caught in a washing machine's ringer. Our neighborhood gang of candidates for remedial classes and reform school also included Shorty, Candy, and Curly from the black families renting run-down houses up by the scrap yard.

The B movies had become an important part of my multicultural awareness—they taught me to hate all those "slant-eyed foreigners" and "red-skinned devils"—but my parents added to the mix by warning me about "the coloreds," who should have been living across the river in the segregated Hill district with "their own kind." We may have been society's unfit, but my parents claimed that the coloreds were the unclean. I was told never to swap drinks or share food with any of the black kids because they had "cooties" and "ringworm." That's why Curly had that rolled-up nylon stocking on his head. The coloreds even caught and ate the filthy pigeons roosting under the Brady Street Bridge and, worse yet, the diseased catfish lurking in the Monongahela. As far as my parents were concerned, we might as well have been living next to a leper colony.

But propinquity often overcame racial suspicion and fear on Merriman Way. There was a demarcation line in the middle of the alley, separating white and black houses, and I was told never to bring one of the coloreds into our house or go into one of theirs. But, once outside, black or white, hillbillies or chiselers, we played our integrated games of war or cowboys and Indians up and down Merriman and its environs, though you had to be careful to "catch a rabbit," not "a nigger," by the toe when you were choosing up sides. If the word "nigger," "coon," or "spade" slipped out of Joey Chisel's mouth in the heat of battle, it was usually followed by Shorty telling him "your mama fucked a nigger, that's how you got here, Chisel," and a shoving match and stone throwing that ended our play and re-segregated our block.

It was not uncommon for our games, once they deteriorated into racial taunts, to be broken up by threats, shoves, and hurled missiles, but my back-alley nemesis was white, not black. Jerome and I hated each other from the moment his family moved in a few houses away. We accused each other of cheating at hide-and-seek. At it-tigers, our tags were more like punches. In our games of war, we always sought each other out with clods of dirt and pieces of coal. When Jerome hit me in the side of the face with the fragment of a brick, I return the favor by getting him down on the ground and slashing at his face with my fingernails until he shook free and ran home in tears. Later that afternoon Jerome's mother dragged her scarred and blood-stained son up our stairs and demanded to know "what kind of goddam monster Lil was raisin' for a son." My mother said she taught me "never to take shit from no one" and told Jerome's mother she'd be better off "mindin' her own kind." After they left, my mother didn't say a word to me, but that evening, after I got ready for bed, she took out her scissors and cut my nails.

Dickie Peterson
wearing pink
carnation on
Mother's Day,
circa 1948.

While there was a city playground around the corner, we were content, when we were getting along, with a childhood wonderland that
extended from our alley to the river, at least until we were old enough
to need a ball field for more organized play. On any given day of our
unsupervised and undirected youth, our band of the unfit and the unclean scrambled through Merriman Way's rag piles and scrap heaps,
then climbed over the low wall of the sand and gravel company and
wandered through sand dunes, coal piles, and odd-looking pieces of
heavy equipment on our way to the railroad tracks and the river bank.
With imaginations fed by radio shows, B movies, and cliff-hangers, we
had sand for our desert adventures, chunks of coal and railroad nuggets
for our war games, a weed-infested river bank where imaginary pools
of quicksand were waiting for the unwary, and a foul-smelling river
where sinkholes and river currents were waiting to suck us under.

When we weren't defying disease and death by wading into the

Monongahela, we were gathering new sexual misinformation along its banks, thanks to Tank and his sister Mae, the only mulattos on the block. Tank and Mae were older than the rest of us, and, with their brownish-yellow skin and red-tinted hair, far more exotic, even for our gang. Tank, who deserved his nickname because of his hulking size, claimed he already had sex and had something awful to share with us. The good news was that our "peckers" weren't going to fall off, as our mothers had warned us would happen if we stuck them where they didn't belong. But they were going to get bloody because that's what happened to Tank when he had sex with one of Mae's girl friends. Since none of us knew very much about the female body, including Tank, we listened with amazement to his story and perfectly misunderstood why he pulled up his pants and ran away.

Tank's worldly sister Mae, however, with her long legs and small, pointed breasts, was willing to help us overcome our fears by offering to show us hers if we'd show her ours, but that's as far as she was willing to go. If one of us wanted more, her standard line was to "go fuck your sister," even if you didn't have a sister. I'd already gone along with a female cousin who offered to lift up her dress and show me her underwear if I'd play cut-outs and dolls with her, but Mae was offering too much, too soon.

When Mae decorated the pubic area of her short shorts with her collection of red cellophane strips from cigarette wrappers and asked what it reminded me of, I leered and nodded in ignorant appreciation and budding lust, but I wasn't quite ready for the real thing, at least not yet. I talked a good game in those days, absorbed every dirty joke, and spiked my vocabulary with every dirty word ever uttered on the South Side, but I really had no idea of what I was talking about except in my distorted imagination. Mae was right when she called me "a little horny toad," but I was suspicious, thanks to Tank, of what Mae was offering and, toad or no toad, fully prepared to run away in a panic if our sex games became too real. It would take a few more years before games of strip poker and truth or dare would become the portals to sexual discovery.

While Tank and Mae, the Kinseys of my childhood, were adding sexual confusion to my B-movie fantasies, I was also learning something about basic economics at home and as I roamed up and down the

My sister, Nancy,
with local bookie,
circa 1950.

South Side. My mother's way of coping with our daily money problems was her hopeless hope that she would hit it big on the numbers. I can still see our numbers runner, tousled-hair Vic, with his small pad in hand, sitting at our kitchen table as if he were family and waiting to write down my mother's usual assortment of penny straights and nickel combinations on the race or the stock. When he was done, he'd hand my mother the carbon copy of her numbers for the day, collect the coins covering her bets, and tell her he'd be back tomorrow with "a handful of bucks" because he could feel it in his "Blue-tail bones" that Lil's number was "gonna come up big today." Vic just knew my mother's "luck was gonna change, just you wait and see, Lil." But my mother, who rarely hit the numbers, would shoo Vic out the door and tell him not to trip on his "lyin' Blue-tail tongue" as he ran down the stairs and headed for his next customer.

America may have been going through a postwar boom on its way into the 1950s and Pittsburgh may have begun its own postwar renaissance, but Uncle Sam and Pa Pitt seemed to have overlooked the South Side, especially the Peterson family. You were better off than most families on the South Side if your father had a union job at the Duquesne brewery, Gimbels warehouse, or the J & L steel mill, but I can still remember walking by freezing Gimbels' strikers huddled around flaming barrels as I hurried on my way to and from Humboldt in the dead of winter. I learned from my striking uncles, who drove delivery trucks and labored on the warehouse docks, that there were rocks inside the snowballs flung at workers crossing the picket line, and that you should "never forget the face of a scab" because he was taking the food from your family's table. My uncles also explained how important it was to vote for Mayor David Lawrence and the Democratic machine because they were for the unions. Mayor Lawrence was booed at every Pirates home opener because most Pittsburghers thought he was as crooked as the hilly Pittsburgh landscape, but Lawrence and his cronies won every election by a landslide, thanks to the city's working class.

My way of sharing in the city's graft and filling my own empty pockets was to become a petty thief. On the South Side it was easy stealing candy bars, comic books, or packs of baseball cards, especially if you had a buddy with you. We'd stroll into Ross's or Breitweiser's confectionery on Carson Street, browse a bit at the counters, then one of us would distract the owner while the other slipped baseball cards inside the pockets of his dungarees or stuffed comic books under his jersey. If one of us had a dime, he'd buy a comic book, fold it in half, then let the other drop Hershey or Clark bars into the folded comic book as we walked out of the store.

By the sixth grade, I'd widened the circle of my petty thievery by occasionally playing hooky from Humboldt with one of my buddies and spending the day wandering around Downtown Pittsburgh, just looking for something to steal from the department stores or the five-and-tens. My life as a shoplifter went undetected until my mother found two glass figurines I'd hidden in my toy box in the attic after lifting them from a Woolworth's floor display. She made it clear that she "damn well" wasn't going to put up with my stealing: "It's bad enough with your dad's boozin', but we ain't no family of thieves." If I kept it up, I was "gonna end up in Juvenile Court" just like Joey Chisel and the rest of the punks on the South Side. She made me get rid of the figurines, which I ditched down a corner sewer, but every time I walked past the corner by Kalki's beer joint, I wondered if my fabulous unicorn and dragon were still down there in the black water and sludge.

Despite my mother's warning, my career as a petty thief continued until I made the mistake of pocketing a fountain pen I found lying in the groove next to the inkwell on my sixth-grade homeroom desk. The pen looked exactly like the one I'd won on a quiz show and lost a few weeks later. Unfortunately, when I got back to my homeroom from recess, Miss McWhorter, who had the shape of a walrus, cheeks like painted turds, and a well-earned reputation for being the meanest teacher at Humboldt, sarcastically announced to the class that a pen was missing. Before we went off to music, she wanted us to search through our desks and pencil boxes just in case one of us "put it away by mistake." She wanted me to take a good look through my things because the boy who lost the pen had sat at my desk during his reading class. Taking a lesson from Bogart, Cagney, and the Dead End Kids, I decided that street cunning, not confession, was the best way out of my jam. As my classmates lifted the lids of their desks in quiet indignation— they knew who had the pen and so did Miss McWhorter—I slipped my free hand into the front pocket of my dungarees, carefully palmed and pulled out the fountain pen, and slid it under the front cover of my reader. I raised my hand, stood up from my desk, and opened the reader. I pulled out the pen in my best Jack Horner manner, and loudly proclaimed, "I found it, Miss McWhorter."

After handing the pen over, I sat down, fully expecting some trapdoor, right out a Saturday matinee chapter, to open under my chair and drop me into a pit of molten lava. But all I got was a burning sensation in my ears as Miss McWhorter mockingly told the class what a good boy I was. But Miss McWhorter was not going to pass up the opportunity to remind her class of the fate of the character in Jack London's "To Build a Fire," one of the stories we'd just finished in our reader. Here was the perfect moment to remind an unfit class, just a few months away from leaving Humboldt, "about the foolish young man who froze to death because he was too smart for his own good and wouldn't listen to those who tried to warn him that he was heading for danger."

The only perceivable danger looming for me at the beginning of the 1950s was going into the seventh grade at South High in September. As far as my life on the South Side was concerned, I probably was too street-smart for my own good, but I didn't think the hardships, struggles, and uncertainties of my working-class parents were cause for rejection or rebellion. My father drank too much and couldn't hold a steady job, but the endless beer joints up and down the South Side were a testament to the alcoholism and chronic unemployment that seemed the inevitable circumstances of working-class life. I felt bad for my mother when my father was out on a bender, but I liked spending my weekend evenings with my father in Kalki's beer joint, watching the fights, wrestling, and roller derby. I spent so much time in Kalki's that I knew the bartender as well as I knew my own uncles and was as comfortable on a barstool as I was on a bike or roller skates.

My poor father was just a grown-up, dead-end kid. He was a terrific mechanic and had an amazing gift for figures, but, working in gas stations, he never had a chance to do much more than thumb the right coins out of his changer. He brooded and drank his Iron City beer far into the night, but his way of dealing with whatever was tormenting him rarely went beyond his black moods. If aroused, he could lacerate the spirit with his words, but he never raised a hand against his family. On his worst days, he'd walked into Kalki's instead of going to work, drink himself into a public spectacle as he reeled from beer joint to beer joint, and stagger his way home in urine-soaked pants, if he could make it at all. On his best days, he went to work, brought home his pay, and occasionally, after supper, played catch with me and talked about the Pirates.

My mother thought my father, with his Clark Gable mustache and slicked-back hair, was quite a catch, even though she had to hock her wedding ring from time to time to get him out of trouble. Her story of the clever, dashing young man with more than one girlfriend, however, was hard to believe when I sat at the kitchen table and looked across at my father's inflamed, ravaged face and his yellow, nicotine-stained fingers. I also had trouble seeing my mother as the "wild thing" who ran off to West Virginia to marry my father.

Years later I learned my mother sometimes went out drinking in the morning after finishing her ten-hour graveyard shift as a waitress and once got on the back of a motorcycle with a customer and went wheeling, waitress uniform and all, up and down Centre Avenue at three in the morning. My mother was a trim, handsome woman with her oval face and "peaches-and-cream" complexion, but the mother I saw leave for work in the evening and wouldn't see again until I got home from school the next day complained bitterly about her varicose veins. She was so tired when she left the house that the last thing she did was to check her purse to make sure she had her "No-Doz" to get her through the night.

It wasn't an easy or very secure life, but I knew we'd never starve as long as my mother had her steady job, waiting tables at Rodger's. On holidays, thanks to my mother's tips, she always managed to buy gifts and treats in an often-futile effort to make things special for the family. Every Christmas, she'd warn me "not to expect too much" because Santa Claus always seemed to be having a bad year, but Santa usually came through as long as my mother's regulars were feeling generous with their tips during the holidays. It was my father and his holiday benders we had to worry about on Christmas day, and he rarely surprised us by staying sober and behaving himself.

My embittered father's bouts of heavy drinking on holidays were the most painful moments of my childhood, but my mother's Christmas gift of a baseball board game when I was ten-years-old was the most miraculous. The game came with miniature plastic players for each position, a small plastic baseball, and a wooden bat to put the ball in play. The board, with its tan infield, green outfield, and gray warning track, was painted to resemble a major-league ballpark. The outfield was ringed off with white lines into diminishing areas for singles, doubles, and triples and had two small pockets of green marked off in deep left and right center for home runs.

The most magical feature of the board game was the foul areas, where the autographs of major league players had been transferred in white to the green surface of the board. Etched along the third-base and left-field foul line were the autographed names of American League stars—Ted Williams, Joe DiMaggio, Bob Feller, and George Kell—that I'd read about in the paper or seen in Movietone highlight reels. Along the first-base and right-field foul lines were the more familiar names of National League stars—Stan Musial, Warren Spahn, Pee Wee Reese, and Johnny Mize—that I'd watched at Forbes Field. I was thrilled when I saw Pirates slugger Ralph Kiner's autograph and was even happy to see Pirates nemesis Ewell Blackwell's name on the board because Blackwell had given up two home runs to Kiner in the first game that I saw at Forbes Field.

Even my father, as he drank his morning coffee and smoked his Lucky Strikes, seemed taken by the board game. While I used cardboard from a discarded shoe box to construct a scoreboard for the game, he sat at the other end of the kitchen table, figured out that the autographs were from ball players on the 1948 All-Star teams, and identified the unfamiliar American League names on the board, like Zeke Zarilla and Hoot Evers. By early afternoon, game or no game, he told me to "go get a bottle of Iron City" from the cold room, and by late afternoon he was well on his way to ruining another holiday as he demanded the bottle of Seagram's he was sure my mother had hidden away. By the time we went downstairs for supper with my grandparents, he was wondering where my mother got the money for my game unless it was from some "sugar daddy" hanging out at Rodger's. But, no matter where the money came from, I had my baseball board game, and, once we got through all the ugliness and nastiness downstairs, I knew I could spent the rest of the evening eating Christmas treats from my stocking and working on the opening-day line ups for my miniature field of dreams.

As I looked down on my board game and dreamed of growing up and playing for the Pirates some day, I was less than a week away from the beginning of a decade in America of political anxieties, racial divisions, and moral confusion. As for my family, we'd have enough trouble of our own to fill the fifties and didn't need much help from paranoid politicians, hood-wearing segregationists, and moral do-gooders.

Thanks to Humboldt, I'd have my own brave new world of emotional turmoil and insecurities facing me in junior high. My reward for scoring well on standardized tests—my teachers bragged to my incredulous mother that I had an IQ of 144, just "one point below the genius level"—was two double promotions that allowed me to skip a whole grade, but guaranteed I'd be a year younger than all the other new seventh-grade students when I started at South High. Short and skinny for my age, an incurable romantic because of the movies, hopelessly confused about sex, but on the verge of raging hormones and an eruption of acne, I was about to become an emotional misfit among the economically unfit. In my years at South High, I'd become an emotional mess, but I'd have no seductive Natalie Wood to hold my hand and no dedicated Glenn Ford to recognize my untapped potential, lurking just "one point below" the level of genius.

But, in the summer of 1950, after matriculating from Humboldt in June, I had enough distractions to keep me from worrying too much about going to high school in September. As I played war games with my Merriman Way buddies, the North Koreans gave us a real shooting war by invading the South. Every day that summer I studied the maps in the Pittsburgh newspapers in a state of disbelief, while our troops retreated from Taejon to Pusan. By September, however, General Mac-Arthur had restored my faith in war by ordering a surprise amphibian assault on Inchon harbor near Seoul that began a rout of the enemy forces and drove them deep into North Korea, all the way to the Yalu River and the border of Communist China, and to the edge of what seemed a certain victory.

The day after Labor Day, with all the ignorance and gullibility of a war-loving eleven-year-old, I headed down Carson Street for my first day at South High. I had no idea how badly things would turn out in Korea or how turbulent the decade would become in American politics. I also didn't have a clue to the personal upheaval I'd be going through in high school, though I had picked up some survival skills on the South Side and at Humboldt. As naive as I was about the world beyond my neighborhood, I was beginning to learn that cunning would serve me well in a working-class environment that valued strong arms and thick skulls over brains.

I was also learning that loyalty to friends, family, community, and, above all, the city's sports teams was an essential part of life on the South Side, though the teams of that decade were often so hapless that they seemed to add to the pain and frustrations of growing up.

But, even if defeats were far more frequent than victories, when the Pirates or the Steelers won a game, it elevated the day no matter what the circumstances of my life. They were my Pirates and Steelers, and their struggles suited the character of my neighborhood and town. I followed their misfortunes with the fanaticism of a true fan, worshipped bumbling ballplayers as if they were larger-than-life heroes, and, without quite knowing it, was beginning to see sports as a way of imagining a world beyond the closed circle of the South Side.

Chapter 3

I don't remember how young I was at the time, but it's easy to see why my first memory of growing up on Pittsburgh's working-class South Side is so vivid. I'm dressed in an Indian outfit, my mother's lipstick streaked on my face for war paint, my headband displaying one proud feather for bravery. As "Pop Goes the Weasel" plays somewhere in the background, I stalk around two diminishing rows of wooden chairs with other costumed children, anticipating the moment when the music stops. It's great fun diving into a chair, laughing when some disappointed cowboy or cowgirl, GI Joe or nurse, hobo or fairy princess walks off the floor. But then it happens, the first defining moment of my childhood. The music stops, I scramble for a chair, and one little Indian is eliminated from the game—or, as I clearly recall, one tantrum-throwing little Indian. My reaction to losing was to break out in a howling rage and fling myself to the floor.

As my embarrassed mother and aunt dragged me out of the bingo hall and yelled at me for being such a "crybaby" and a "poor sport," I was about to enter a working-class world of school and play where friendships and rivalries were established and defined by the way you competed in games. I was also on the way to becoming a bad-tempered loser just as Pittsburgh's post–World War II baseball and football teams were on the threshold of becoming the worst teams in professional sports. Losing at musical chairs was just the beginning of a boy's life in which playing at games, rather than a diversion, would become the way of finding identity and pride in a world hostile to the spirit of youth. And as I played ball as if my life depended on it, rooting for

Pittsburgh's sports teams became the way of sustaining some dream or hope of a life beyond steel mills and coal fields, even if the teams were as hopeless as the dream itself.

So many of my memories of Pittsburgh in the late 1940s and early 1950s are of playing ball on grassless city fields and poorly surfaced courts and hitchhiking out to Forbes Field, Pitt Stadium, or the Duquesne Gardens to watch the city's sports teams. The seasons of my youth on the South Side flowed by to the rhythm of games played with baseballs and bats held together with masking tape and nails, footballs made of newspapers folded and tied with twine, hockey sticks pieced back together after being shattered and abandoned at Hornets games, and slick-surfaced basketballs often lopsided and bubbled from too much wear. In the spring and summer I lived to play softball around the corner at Ormsby playground and baseball up the hill at Quarry Field, and I died watching the rinky-dink Pirates lose game after game. In the autumn I turned to school yard and alley football and followed the same old Steelers, at least until life and sports fell off into the dark winter days. Then I reluctantly followed minor-league hockey and college basketball, roller-skated badly on abandoned tennis courts, dribbled away the hours at poorly heated church gyms, and waited for spring.

Poet laureate Donald Hall once claimed that a love for baseball begins with a father playing catch with his son: "Baseball is fathers and sons playing catch, lazy and murderous, wild and controlled, the profound archaic song of birth, growth, age, and death." This simple act of a father and son playing catch has become a revered image for generations of baseball fans and a powerful metaphor in baseball films and books for the emotional bond between generations. Both *The Natural* and *Field of Dreams,* two of baseball's most popular movies, end with the image of a father playing catch with his son. Even the irreverent *Bull Durham* features a veteran minor-league catcher who has to teach a childlike pitcher how to grow up on his way to the big leagues.

Many of baseball's best writers claim that their books were inspired by memories of their fathers. In his groundbreaking oral history, *The Glory of Their Times,* Lawrence Ritter wrote that, by going back into baseball's past, he was trying "to draw closer to a father [he] would never see again." In *The Boys of Summer,* often praised as baseball's best-written book, Roger Kahn claimed that at the heart of his history of the Brooklyn Dodgers of the 1950s was the emotional relationship with his father: "the bond between my father and me was baseball."

I have my own strong memories of playing catch with my father—when we had time for each other—but they stand out, not because of some Field of Dreams moment. Playing catch gave me a chance to spend some time with a man who seldom had anything to say to me. Rather than cherished moments of magical exchanges and youthful discoveries, my baseball memories of my father stand out because they were the times he was willing to talk about the few things that mattered to him in a life clouded by alcohol.

On those few occasions when we played catch, my father would gradually open up about his own boy's life on the South Side. As we tossed the ball back and forth, he talked about his good old days when he pitched for a Lithuanian team that went up and down the South Side playing against rival "Polacks, Hunkies, and Serbs." He told stories about his younger brother Tony, who was called "Mustard Face" because he loved his mustard sandwiches as much as he loved baseball, and his older brother Joe, who was called "Joky" because he loved his cards and dice more than playing ball. My father told me not to worry about being "so goddam short and skinny" because he was "pretty puny lookin'" in his own day. If I took my mother's advice and "stayed away from the booze" when I grew up, I wouldn't end up with my old man's "beer belly" and high blood pressure, and, if I paid attention, I might learn a few things about throwing drops and in-shoots and maybe turn out some day to be a damn good pitcher like young Frankie Petrauskas was a long time ago.

I don't recall my age when my father and I played our first game of catch, but he started taking me to Pirates games at Forbes Field in 1948 when I was nine years old. It was the beginning, win or lose, and mostly they lost, of a lifelong love affair with my hometown Pirates. We'd usually go out to a Saturday afternoon game, though before we left the house I had to endure my father's ritual-like preparation for attending the game. I remember trying not to fidget as my father finished his black coffee and Lucky Strike. I impatiently watched him shave at the kitchen sink, trim his mustache, and put on a clean white shirt as he explained to me, "We can't look like bums if we're goin' to the game. Wait till you see how people dress. Men in suits and ties. Women all dressed up in fancy hats."

"It's like goin' to church," he added, "though I ain't been to church since I married your mom. The priests don't like it when you marry outta faith, but who the hell cares what they think. Right, Dickie?"

After my father was ready, I had to endure the humiliation of my mother wetting a comb and fussing with my hair, as she slipped a dollar "for a souvenir" in my pocket and kept telling me to stay close to my father because it was Saturday and "there's gonna be a big crowd at the ballpark." As my father and I headed up the alley, I can still hear her yelling to "watch your step and stick to your old man" and for my father to "keep the kid outta the beer joints and make sure he gets somethin' to eat at the game." My mother didn't have to worry about my eating something—I was ready to stuff my face with hotdogs until I puked—but there was no way my father was going to the ballpark without having a beer or two along the way.

Despite my mother's warning, getting out to Forbes Field with my father was always an adventure because we first had to stop at Kalki's around the corner for a beer and a Coke before we caught the street-car out to the game. When we finally made it out to the ballpark, we also had to stop at the Home Plate Café because they didn't sell beer inside Forbes Field in those days. Once inside, I watched the Pirates and listened to my father talk baseball at least until the seventh-inning stretch, which was usually my father's signal to head back to the Home Plate Café, where I was to join him after the game was over.

The Pirates were rapidly becoming my bumbling boys of summer, but at least for a while I had my father's stories as proof that there was a time—maybe long ago, but a time—when ballplayers in a Pirates uniform could actually play baseball. It also helped to have two Pirates legends, Honus Wagner and Pie Traynor, living in Pittsburgh when I first started rooting for the Pirates. The bow-legged and barrel-chested Wagner, who grew up in Pittsburgh's Carnegie area, was such a beloved figure that he became the first Pirate honored with a statue, unveiled outside of Forbes Field at the beginning of the 1951 season, just months before Wagner's death. A part-time Pirate coach after he retired, Wagner loved to tell tales about his playing days. "The Flying Dutchman," who had hands like shovels, claimed he was playing shortstop one day and scooped up

Forbes Field, home of the Pirates and the Steelers, circa 1960 (courtesy of the Pittsburgh Pirates)

a rabbit with the baseball. He hesitated but still managed to throw the runner out "by a hare." The tale was a groaner, but it was perfect for young fans who believed that baseball players were folk heroes.

Honus Wagner was before my father's time, but, as a young fan, he'd watched the great third baseman Pie Traynor, who was elected to the Baseball Hall of Fame in 1948, the same year that I saw my first Pirate game at Forbes Field. With his New England accent and his distinguished silver-haired appearance, Traynor was the closest thing we had in Pittsburgh to baseball royalty, but he also had the common touch with Pirates fans. After his career as player and manager, Traynor became a part-time scout for the Pirates, but he also spent time as a sportscaster on one of the local radio stations. In the early days of television, he became a popular pitchman for American Heating and made regular Saturday appearances on studio wrestling. My father may have seen Pie Traynor in the glory of his times, but my fondest memory of Traynor is on a snowy black-and-white TV, asking Pittsburgh, "Who can? Ameri-can!"

While Wagner and Traynor were around to remind me of past Pirate greatness, I also had the opportunity to watch games at Forbes Field, one of the first steel and concrete palaces, built in 1909 as baseball entered its modern age. Though Forbes Field has since gone the way of the wrecking ball, I can still see the mammoth, aging ballpark as if it were the eighth wonder of the world. In my eyes, it was the biggest, best damn-looking ballpark in baseball. To get a sense of its beauty, all I had to do was look out at the Pitt Cathedral looming majestically behind the left-field bleachers and at the trees in Schenley Park surrounding the red-bricked outfield wall. To get a feel for its size, I could look out at the deep recesses in center field and at the iron gates in right-center where fans walked out of the ballpark at the end of the game.

Forbes Field wasn't some bandbox like Ebbets Field with its gaudy signs or like the Polo Grounds with its cigar shape and its cheap "Chinese home runs." Even after the Pirates put in the Greenberg Gardens and shortened left field by thirty feet to help sluggers Hank Greenberg and Ralph Kiner hit home runs, Forbes Field still had plenty of room for doubles down the lines and triples in the alleys. Center field was so deep that the grounds crew rolled the batting cage out to the 457 mark and it rarely interfered with a game. And even when Barney Dreyfuss, the Pirate owner who built Forbes Field, had to shorten right field for a new grandstand, he put up a high screen down the right-field line to prevent cheap home runs. Forbes Field wasn't built for home-run hitters, but the ballpark was a line-drive hitter's paradise with all its open space. No pitcher, not even the great Dizzy Dean or Carl Hubbell, had ever pitched a no-hitter at Forbes Field, and no pitcher ever would.

I'm glad my father had his proud memories of Pirates past because, when I looked down with him from the bleachers or the grandstands at Forbes Field, we saw a Pirates team on its way to becoming one of the worst in baseball. It was a good thing that my father quit going to games with me after I was old enough to get out to the ballpark by myself because the Pirates in the early 1950s were the joke of the National League. After finishing last in 1950, the Pirates hired the legendary Branch Rickey to run the team and, like Stalin's Soviet Union, they embarked on a disastrous five-year plan that doomed Pittsburgh fans to an emotional Siberia. With baseball mastermind Rickey leading the way, the Pirates came in next to last in 1951, Rickey's first year in Pittsburgh, then, after Rickey boastfully declared, "We're pointing to 1955. That's when the bells will start ringing as the red wagon comes down the street," the Pirates finished dead last for the next four years.

Desperate for success after being forced out of Brooklyn, Rickey was ready to trade anyone to any team willing to deal with him. He got rid of popular players like no-hit pitcher Cliff Chambers and hard-hitting outfielders Wally Westlake and Gus Bell for the likes of bespectacled infielder Dick Cole, who should have worn his glove on his shin, prematurely bald Joe Garagiola, who discovered in last place Pittsburgh that "baseball is a funny game," and banjo-hitting Johnny Berardino, who parlayed a trip to the Pirates minor league Hollywood Stars into a successful acting career in television soap operas.

By 1952 I was a diehard, thirteen-year-old, knothole-gang member, and a witness to a Pirate team that was so awful it became the stuff of legend. Manager Bill Meyer was so disgusted that he told his players, "You clowns can go on 'What's My Line?' in full uniform and stump the panel." One of baseball's all-time disasters, the 1952 Pirates, the infamous "Rickey Dinks," ended the season with a woeful record of 42–112, the worst in modern franchise history. My favorite pitcher, poor Murry Dickson, lost twenty-one games as the leader of a staff that used up twenty pitchers, fourteen of them finishing a collective 5–38 for the year. The twenty-six position players included two nineteen-year-old rookies fresh out of Pittsburgh high schools. First baseman Tony Bartirome, destined to become a Pirates trainer after lasting one year in the major leagues, and center fielder Bobby Del Greco combined for one home run on a team so terrible that Joe Garagiola described it as "a ninth-place ball club in an eight-team league."

Home-run king and future Hall of Famer Ralph Kiner was the only bright spot for the Pirates in 1952, but he was a sore spot for Branch Rickey, who had a much-deserved reputation for being a tightwad. Kiner's home runs may have been the reason a handful of sorrowful Pirates fans still came out to Forbes Field, but Rickey didn't see it that way. As far as he was concerned, the Pirates finished last in 1952 with Kiner and his big salary, and they could damn well finish last in 1953 without him. Rickey's solution, after denigrating Kiner in the press for being pampered and spoiled, was to offer Kiner to Chicago in a ten-player deal that included Garagiola and two other Pirates for six Cubs and $150,000.

On June 4, 1953, when Rosey Rowswell sent word of the Kiner trade out over the radio just before the game between the Pirates and the Cubs, I felt betrayed by Rickey. Growing up in a working-class neighborhood, I

Childhood idol Ralph Kiner, circa 1948 (courtesy of the Pittsburgh Pirates)

saw Kiner as a baseball god. Short and skinny, I dreamed that someday I might become a wily pitcher like Murry Dickson, but Ruthian Kiner was beyond my baseball fantasies. I cocked my right elbow at the plate and swung with an uppercut, just like Kiner, but I knew that Kiner's towering home runs were the stuff of the Mighty Casey and Ozark Ike. Playing in a shot-and-a-beer, steel-mill town, Kiner was strictly Hollywood. Saying "Fords were for singles hitters," he drove Cadillacs, dated starlets, including Elizabeth Taylor, and eventually married tennis professional Nancy Chaffee, who was often seen parading around decaying Forbes Field with her leashed Afghan hounds.

If baseball in the 1950s had a Shakespeare looking to write about a star-crossed team, he could have turned to the Pirates and found plenty of material. Before and after the Kiner trade, the Pirates were the stuff of theater, though mostly low comedy. They even became the subject of a 1951 Hollywood movie, *Angels in the Outfield,* in which a hapless Pirates team, led by a foul-mouthed, brawling manager played by Paul Douglas, becomes a pennant winner when the angelic spirits of baseball greats descend upon Forbes Field to help win games—as long as the manager keeps his temper. Several of the Pirates made cameo appearances in the movie, and Kiner managed to have a brief affair with Douglas's costar, Janet Leigh, but the filmmakers probably had to use stuntmen when one of the Pirates made a great play.

With no angels or stuntmen in the outfield or anywhere else at Forbes Field, my most vivid memories of Rickey's Pirates, as they finished last in 1953 without Kiner and last again in 1954 and 1955, are of inept players and ridiculous plays. There were all those bonus babies and rookie phenoms who should have been arrested for fraud after putting on big-league uniforms. The Pirates signed the basketball All-American O'Brien twins, who flopped badly, and acquired the brothers Freese, who also failed to double the pleasure of Pirate fans. When not signing teenagers, Rickey picked up aging veterans better suited for an old-timers game, like ex-Yankee slugger Johnny Lindell, who was trying to hang on, without much success, as a knuckle-ball pitcher, and ex-Yankee World Series hero Joe Page, who had an astronomical earned run average in his one hazy, alcoholic season with the Pirates.

While my father grew up watching Hall of Famer Pie Traynor, I'm stuck with vivid nightmares of Gene Freese pulling a Merkle boner and costing the Pirates a rare victory by failing to run down and touch second base on what should have been a game-winning hit; of Tommy Saffell turning to play a ball off the outfield wall as the ball landed beside him; and of Danny Kravitz failing to catch a foul pop up behind home plate because he didn't have a catcher's mitt glued to the top of his head. I listened to broadcaster Rosey Rowswell moan about his "achin' back" as he recreated Pirate road losses from ticker-tape accounts of the games, and, on one unforgettable occasion in 1956, after high school baseball practice, heard Bob Prince describe, in a voice of disbelief, the last inning of a game from Wrigley Field in which Sad Sam Jones completed a no-hitter against the Pirates by walking the first three batters, then striking out three Pirates, including Roberto Clemente, to end the game.

My father quit taking me to see the Pirates once I was old enough to find my own way out to Forbes Field, but he still listened to Rosey Rowswell and Bob Prince on the radio and watched televised games from his stool at Kalki's. Clinging to his own baseball memories, he could no more desert the Pirates than a devoted parent could give up on a child who keeps getting beat up by bullies and keeps bringing home a bad report card from school. But the Pittsburgh Steelers were another matter. My father loved college football and talked with pride about Jock Sutherland's great Pitt Panther teams, and "what a goddam shame it was, Sutherland dyin' of a brain tumor" in early 1948, just two years after taking over the Steelers for Art Rooney. But he refused to spend the money to take me out to Forbes Field for a Steelers game because he thought professional football "ain't always on the up and up." He took me to Kalki's to watch the fights on the Gillette Cavalcade of Sports and the Pabst Blue Ribbon Bouts, and we even watched pro wrestling, which was as phony as Gorgeous George. But he was not going to spend money on the Steelers because, as long as pro football used referees from the same region as the home team, the Steelers were "gonna get jobbed" every time they played on the road.

Occasionally the Steelers justified my father's cynicism by losing a close road game on a questionable call, but the Steelers of my youth usually didn't need much help from referees to lose football games. They weren't as awful as the Pirates, but they were consistent losers, the "same old Steelers"—a hard-luck team bought in 1933 for $2,500 out of Art Rooney's legendary racetrack winnings and plagued for decades by Rooney's cronyism. The Pirates may have bumbled their way through my South Side childhood, but the Steelers, even with some good players and a few great ones, managed to bungle every opportunity for a championship.

In 1941, after enduring eight straight losing seasons, Art Rooney, in response to a newspaper contest, changed his football team's name from the Pirates to the Steelers. When asked by a reporter what he thought of his newly christened Steelers, Rooney answered, "They looked like the same team to me." They finished 1–9–1 for the year. That tag, the "same old Steelers," would hang around Rooney's neck like a deflated football for the next three decades, and for good reason. In the 1950s pro football entered the golden age of television with revolutionized T-formation offenses led by Sammy Baugh, Otto Graham, Bob Waterfield, and Bobby Layne, but the Steelers, stuck in the 1930s, still ran the obsolete single wing. One of the most popular advertisements in Pittsburgh at the beginning of the 1950s was an arrangement of eleven bottles of Duquesne pilsner in a single-wing formation. The Steelers hold the historical distinction of being the last pro football team to use the single wing long after other teams abandoned it.

When the Steelers finally installed the T-formation, they still seemed like the same old Steelers because they developed the most predictable T-formation offense in pro football. They opened each game with the same play so often—a handoff to fullback Fran Rogel—that Pittsburgh fans, including one angry kid from the South Side, chanted, " Hi diddle diddle, Rogel up the middle" when the Steelers broke huddle and approached the line of scrimmage for their first offensive series.

Rooney's same old Steelers may have been the misfits of pro football in the 1950s, but they were the perfect misfits for a hard-fisted steel town. They actually were fun to watch at times, even when they were losing, because their defense was mean and tough and routinely beat the hell out of other teams. Ernie Stautner, the only same-old-Steeler to make it into the Hall of Fame, wore makeshift casts on his hands, even though they weren't broken, so he could pound offensive linemen into submission. The Steelers' games against Norm "Wild Man" Willey and their state-rival Philadelphia Eagles were bloodbaths, where more players made it to the emergency room than into the end zone.

Commissioner Bert Bell once warned the two teams against using their "forearms, elbows, or knees" to maim their opponents, a warning that was ignored at game time. On one memorable Saturday evening in 1955, the Steelers, with quarterback Jim Finks wearing a catcher's mask on the front of his helmet to protect the broken jaw he suffered in an earlier game in Philadelphia, put several Eagles in the hospital, won the game in dramatic fashion, and took over first place in the NFL's Eastern Division. But the Steelers were so banged up after beating the Eagles that they lost six of their last seven games and ended up with another losing season.

The other intense Steelers rivalry, though it was usually one-sided on the scoreboard, was with the Cleveland Browns. Unlike the brawling Steelers, the Browns were all smugness and precision. While Stautner managed to put a few dents in Paul Brown's pride and joy, the Browns pretty much named the score against the Steelers. One of my best Forbes Field memories is looking down at Otto Graham screaming at his offensive linemen, including future Steelers coach Chuck Noll, because the Steelers were knocking down Graham on every pass play. But one of my worst Forbes Field memories is watching Marion Motley, after losing his helmet on a missed tackle, run through or bounce off the entire Steelers defense on his way to a touchdown. After the lopsided game, Motley boasted that running against the Steelers was "like runnin' downhill."

The Steelers of my boyhood were not satisfied just to brawl their way out of contention each year. Their off-the-field bungling more than matched their on-the-field losses. This was a team that occasionally drafted great college football players but cut them because they couldn't recognize their obvious talent. More often, they passed over great players to make incredibly bad choices in the draft or simply traded away high draft choices for another team's castoffs.

Their biggest blunder, however, became the stuff of pro football legend. In 1955, the year of Roberto Clemente's rookie season with the Pirates, the Steelers drafted Louisville quarterback Johnny Unitas, a Lithuanian kid who grew up in a Pittsburgh working-class neighborhood and played high school football against one of Art Rooney's sons. But the Steelers coaches thought Unitas was too dumb to be a pro football quarterback and cut him a week before the season opener. Unitas ended up playing sandlot football in Pittsburgh for the Bloomfield Rams until he got a call from the Baltimore Colts, where he played the next seventeen years and was smart enough to win three world championship games, including the 1958 overtime thriller that, thanks to television, turned pro football into a rival to baseball as America's most popular sport.

Undaunted, the Steelers finally seemed to catch a break the next year when they hit pro football's jackpot and won the bonus draft pick for 1956. Year after year, I waited for the Steelers to win the bonus pick, and with only two teams left in the lottery, the Steelers and the Lions, Rooney, who couldn't lose at the racetrack and couldn't win for the Steelers, finally pulled the right slip out of Commissioner Bert Bell's hat. At last my same old Steelers were poised to change their luck and their history. There were wonderful draft picks, great running backs waiting for the Steelers, like Ohio State Heisman Trophy winner Howard "Hopalong" Cassady and Penn State All-American Lenny Moore. But when the announcement came, the Steelers, to my disbelief and my father's "I-told-you-so," drafted somebody named Gary Glick out of some place called Colorado A&M. Drafting Glick as a quarterback after the Unitas fiasco, the Steelers discovered that he may have been smart enough to play the position, but he couldn't pass worth a damn. Glick spent three mediocre years with Pittsburgh playing defensive back, while failing miserably as a placekicker.

My father may have been content to spend his Sundays in the fall drinking beer and playing poker at the Duquesne Social Club while Joe Tucker's broadcast of Steelers games droned on in the background, but I was determined to be at Forbes Field for their home games. Win or lose, they were my same old Steelers. Getting money for Pirates games on Sunday was never a problem—I'd bum a dollar from my mother's Saturday night tips, get her to pack a bag full of chipped ham sandwiches, throw in a large bottle of Tom Tucker pop, and I was all set to spend a long, sun-burned afternoon in the left-field bleachers, watching the Pirates lose a doubleheader. I also had all those free Saturday knot-hole games, as thousands of us watched from the right-field stands and usually outnumbered the paying customers. But a Steelers ticket cost three times as much as a Pirates ticket and was too steep for my mother's tips, even if she'd had a good night. So my football buddies and I had to come up with a plan to get into Forbes Field for nothing.

During the 1950s, I saw almost every Steelers home game and didn't pay a dime. I got up Sunday morning and conned my mother into believing I was going out to Forbes Field early to see the Steelers if I could get into the game by peddling the Sunday papers. I pleaded with her to pack me a lunch just in case, smuggled some old newspapers under my coat, and headed out to the ballpark. Once I met up with my football buddies, our ranks slightly depleted by the Catholics who couldn't talk their way out of Sunday Mass, we made our way out to Oakland and headed into Schenley Park, where we walked around the outer wall of Forbes Field until we got to the iron gates. With the ballpark still unguarded, we found a Schenley Park bench and propped it against the outfield wall so that the bench legs served as a ladder. We climbed up the bench, avoided the barbwire fringing the top of the outfield wall, walked a tightrope along the ledge, and took a football leap of faith into the deserted right-field grandstands.

Once inside Forbes Field and with nearly two hours to kill before the ticket gates opened, we had to go somewhere to avoid the police and ushers who would soon be patrolling the ballpark. After exploring the rusted underground of Forbes Field, we eventually came across the perfect hideaway, perfect if you didn't mind utter darkness, absolute filth, and the sound of rats scurrying a few yards away from where you were hiding. Our black hole, where we disappeared until the gates opened at noon, existed beneath the right-field stands where the back wall of a storage shed for ballpark concessions intersected the slanted underbelly of the grandstand and left a small opening just big enough for a handful of working-class fugitives to crawl through and escape detection. Once through the hole, we spread out old newspapers to lie on and swore "not to make a goddam peep" so workers loading up supplies for the concession stands wouldn't hear us. We threatened " to beat the shit" out of the first one that farted and waited until the sound of chains and rolling metal alerted us that the gates were opening and law-abiding ticket holders were about to enter the ballpark.

Emerging from our tomblike sanctuary, after praying for what seemed an eternity that the workers wouldn't hear us moving about to get comfortable and the rats wouldn't confuse our toes with the lunches they were no doubt smelling, we must have appeared an unholy sight to the paying Steelers fans dressed in their Sunday finest. With our clothes smudged with newspaper print, our hands and knees caked with filth, and our hair and caps coated with spider webs, we must have looked like escaped waifs from some western Pennsylvania coal mine or displaced persons camp. But appearances to the contrary, we were now a part of the Sunday crowd and, after our descent into the underworld, more than ready for another bruising Steelers loss.

The right-field grandstands at Forbes Field were long-distant viewing for baseball, but they offered the best seats in the house for football. Since we had no tickets and the stands were quickly filling up with paying fans, we improvised once again by climbing on top of a concession stand located near the fifty-yard line. From our little crow's nest, we looked down on the same old Steelers, ate our finger-print stained "sammiches," and yelled with all our working-class vehemence and teenage vulgarity for the blood and broken bones of Steelers opponents—for Jack Butler to "break his goddam arms" every time Pete Pihos or Mac Speedie reached out for a pass, for Dale Dodrill to tear the head off "that fuckin' midget" every time Eddie LaBaron scrambled out of the pocket, and for anyone, even Gary Glick, to break the legs of Ollie Matson before he broke free on a kickoff return.

Forbes Field may have been the pleasure palace of my father's youth, but for me it was part amusement park, part obstacle course, and part torture chamber. It was also the towering centerpiece of an Oakland sports complex that included Pitt Stadium, the Pitt Field House and the Duquesne Gardens. Oakland, just a forty-minute walk from my South Side neighborhood, was where I could escape from the boredom of public school and the unhappiness of family life, learn how to connive and hustle my way to the objects of my heart's desire, and gain early lessons about loyalty, toughness, and even pride in a hard-nosed city closely identified with smoke, soot, and losing professional sports teams. Palatial Forbes Field and its major-league sports dominated my boyhood fantasies and adventures from April to December, but I also had the chance to hitchhike to Oakland and watch games at Pitt Stadium in the fall and at Duquesne Gardens in the winter. It meant following college football and basketball and minor-league hockey, but, while the Pirates and the Steelers played like amateurs and bush leaguers, the Pitt Panthers, Duquesne Dukes, and the Pittsburgh Hornets actually had winning teams in the 1950s.

I never bothered trying to penetrate the concrete bowl of Pitt Stadium because I either got into the game on a high school pass or could watch Pitt football for nothing if I didn't mind missing 30 percent of the game. By standing on a hill overlooking the north end zone, I could see the action from the south end zone, across midfield, to about the thirty-yard line, where players and the game disappeared under the outer rim of the stadium. I saw Corny Salvaterra option Pitt into the Sugar Bowl and the Gator Bowl in 1955 and 1956, but half of his touchdown runs and passes at Pitt Stadium were invisible to my eyes, validated only by the roar of the crowd and sportscaster Ray Scott screaming on somebody's portable radio, "It's a touchdown. What a great play. You had to see it to believe it." I groaned as Penn State's Lenny Moore and Syracuse's Jim Brown broke off dazzling open-field runs, only to watch them disappear once they crossed Pitt's thirty-yard line. And I looked down in disbelief as Freddy Wyant led West Virginia to a great 17–0 upset over Pitt in 1955, though in my mind's eye some of his passes are still waiting to be caught.

The West Virginia upset is still a vivid memory because of what happened when my football buddies and I went into the stadium, as we usually did after a game, to play tackle football on the thick grass carpet. As we were leaving the field, we stumbled across the discarded crossbar from the goal post torn down by Mountaineer fans who had come up from Morgantown for the game. Like bearers of forgotten treasure, we carried the crossbar in triumph down Cardiac Hill to Forbes Avenue, sneaked warily past the Juvenile Court building, and made the long hike high above the Monongahela River and the flaming Jones and Laughlin steel mill to the Brady Street Bridge, where we finally figured out what we were "gonna do with the fuckin' thing." Once we got to the middle of the bridge, we scratched our names, the date, and the score of the game into the crossbar and, shouting "one, two, three," heaved it over the railing. We watched the crossbar plunge into the water, before emerging and floating downriver through industrial slime and human waste to its final resting place. It should have been a trophy on the campus of West Virginia, but, thanks to us, it ended up as a piece of unrecognizable, rotting debris somewhere on the banks of the Monongahela or the Ohio.

While Pitt Stadium may have seemed impenetrable, the Duquesne Gardens, where I watched the minor-league hockey Pittsburgh Hornets and occasionally the college basketball Duquesne Dukes, was a free-loader's paradise. Getting into the run-down Gardens, located several blocks past Forbes Field and Carnegie Tech, was as easy as rapping on a door. Originally built at the turn of the century as a streetcar barn, the Gardens had a series of side exits just waiting for the right moment. All my hockey buddies and I had to do was walk around to the side of the building, knock on one of the metal doors, and hope some paying Hornets fan, remembering his own panhandling youth, would push open the door and let us in for an evening of bruising hockey.

If no one responded or, worse yet, an usher opened the door and told us "to get the hell outta here" before he got a cop, we went over to the building's fire escape and climbed up to the roof. On the top of the Gardens was a small structure resembling a doghouse. We'd swing open the door, lie on our bellies, and look down on the hockey rink. There is no remembered sensation from my South Side youth stranger than looking straight down at the Hornets skating up and down the ice against the Cleveland Barons, Hershey Bears, or Providence Reds with the heat of the arena rising up to warm the upper torso of my body and the bitter cold of a Pittsburgh winter threatening my lower extremities with frostbite. I probably still have all my toes—we wore our battered "tennies" all year round—because some fan would inevitably look up and start pointing at the sight of hockey angels with dirty faces staring down at him. Knowing a cop was soon on the way, we'd bid farewell with our middle finger, beat it back down the fire escape, and start the ritual of rapping on the side doors all over again.

I had no serious interest in basketball because Pittsburgh hadn't owned a professional team since the Ironmen back in the 1940s. But if I got a student pass, I'd trek out to the Steel Bowl tournament at the Pitt Field House or take in the Duquesne Dukes at the old Gardens. Under legendary coach Dudey Moore, the Dukes, who regularly played in the National Collegiate Athletic Association and the National Invitation Tournament (you could play in both until the 1952 season), were one of the best teams in college basketball. With All-Americans Dick Ricketts and

Si Green doing most of the scoring, the Dukes won the NIT in 1955, the same year my South High Orioles won the basketball city championship at the Pitt Field House and advanced to the western regional.

Even the basketball Pitt Panthers, who rarely made it to a postseason tournament, generated some excitement in the 1950s after undersized Don Hennon from Wampum, Pennsylvania, accepted a scholarship at Pitt. For decades, Pitt's only claim to basketball notoriety, as the football Panthers roared to national prominence, was the eccentric behavior of coach Red Carlson, who fed ice cream to his players at half-time and threw peanuts to Pitt students watching the game. But, with Hennon and his soft running hook shot and his brilliant play making, Pitt's basketball team made it to the NCAA tournament in 1957 and 1958. Hennon also brought his own notoriety to Pitt because his father, who was the basketball coach at Wampum, gained national media attention for his unorthodox training drills—his players dribbled blindfolded and ran up and down the court in galoshes. Without his blindfold and galoshes, Hennon was so quick and accurate that I once saw him throw a no-look pass to hatchet man Mike Ditka, who had better luck catching football passes. The ball hit Ditka in the chest, bounced on the fly back to Hennon, who promptly scored a basket on his running jump hook—with the assist, of course, going to Ditka.

When the Duquesne Gardens fell to the wrecking ball in 1956, Pittsburgh's greatest sports loss was that of the Pittsburgh Hornets. The basketball games and the boxing and wrestling matches could find another building, but the Hornets, who came to Pittsburgh in the 1930s as an American Hockey League minor-league franchise, left town and didn't return until the Civic Arena opened in 1961. A farm club for the Toronto Maple Leafs, the Hornets weren't the first professional hockey team to play in Pittsburgh—the National Hockey League Pirates struggled for five years in the late 1920s and finally left after the Depression season of 1929–30 to become the Philadelphia Quakers. But the Hornets were popular in Pittsburgh. Hornets fans, including a half-frozen, top-of-the-world South Sider, were watching minor league hockey, but it was winning hockey. In the early 1950s, the Hornets won several division titles and two Calder Cups, symbols of minor-league hockey supremacy.

The Hornets players weren't big league, but they took on added importance for me because of my mother. My father brought the

Pirates to life for me and the Steelers fit the hard-boiled character of my hometown, but the Hornets belonged to my mother. She didn't understand a thing about hockey, couldn't distinguish a red line from a blue line, but she knew her hockey players because they hung out at Rodger's after home games at the Gardens.

My mother had a wild streak in her and, unlike my brooding father, compensated for the unhappiness of her home life, by having a good time at work. Throughout the early 1950s, she waited booths and flirted with future Hall of Famers George Armstrong and Timmy Horton, who were passing through Pittsburgh on their way to greatness in the National Hockey League, and former Toronto Maple Leafs Wild Bill Ezinicki and Howie Meeker, who were on their last legs with the Hornets. With their toothless smiles and their stitched-up faces, they were my mother's battered boys of winter. Her favorite Hornet, Pete Backor, even promised Lil Peterson's son a hockey stick. She kept telling me "Pete's a good guy. I'm sure he'll get you a stick." But poor Pete Backor, after one glorious season in 1944–45 with the Stanley Cup Champion Maple Leafs, spent the better part of the next decade in Pittsburgh, waiting in vain for another chance to play in the National Hockey League, and poor Dickie Peterson, over fifty years later, is still waiting for his hockey stick.

I spent most of my misplaced youth rooting for two of the worst teams in the history of major-league sports, but the Pirates, in the late 1950s, finally gave me something to cheer about. With gifted players, like Roberto Clemente and Bill Mazeroski, finally maturing into greatness and management willing to trade local favorites for solid veterans, the Pirates actually became a good team. They went on to win the National League pennant in 1960, their first in thirty-three years, and beat Casey Stengel's heavily favored Yankees on Mazeroski's dramatic home run in one of the wildest World Series in baseball history. In the fall of 1960, I snaked and danced my way through Pittsburgh downtown streets in a wild celebration of the Pirates victory, but by next spring the excitement was gone, and the Pirates were back in the doldrums.

The Steelers, giving away draft choices like they were Green Stamps to acquire veteran players, like quarterback Bobby Layne, also made life interesting. With the brash, bloated Layne, who played without a facemask and threw touchdown passes like they were wounded ducks, the Steelers were no longer just the same old Steelers. With the

Pirates radio booth with broadcaster Rosey Rowswell, co-owner Bing Crosby to his right, and Steelers owner Art Rooney standing to his left, circa 1947 (courtesy of the Pittsburgh Pirates)

hard-drinking Layne leading the way, including the way to Pittsburgh nightspots during the week, the Steelers changed their reputation from brawling losers to brawling drunks. In 1963, the year after Layne was forced into retirement, the Steelers were in a position to win their first championship, but they lost to the New York Giants in the last game of the season. After the game, the Steelers lamented their decision a year earlier to retire Layne—and most Steelers fans were ready to drink to that as they drowned their sorrow in Iron City beer.

It wasn't until the 1970s that the Steelers joined the Pirates in giving their long-suffering fans a world championship. By the time the decade was over, the Steelers had won four Super Bowls, and the Pirates added to the glory by winning two World Series. But, because I grew up with Pittsburgh sports in the 1950s, those Pirate Rickey Dinks and the Same Old Steelers are the players I remember most vividly, though the memories are often painful. In a way, they even appear larger than life in my memories. They were the closest thing I had to heroes in an otherwise drab, blue-collar world. They played out their follies at a magnificent ballpark, at one time a symbol of civic pride, but now just a Pittsburgh sports memory. They gave me pride and hope, no matter how foolish and misguided, because they were *my* Pirates and Steelers. No matter how often they disappointed and angered me, they still deserved my loyalty and love because they were all I had. I was thrilled with all the Super Bowl and World Series wins in the 1970s, but my strongest emotions and memories still belong to those bumbling Pirates and brawling Steelers of the 1950s.

Thanks to those misfit teams of Branch Rickey and Art Rooney, I still feel a deep loyalty and pride in the city of my youth. When I was growing up, I hated to lose at anything, but, whether they won or lost, the Pirates and Steelers were the one certainty I had in a life of working-class uncertainties and insecurities. No matter how unhappy or inferior I felt in school or at play, I could always go out to the ballpark and root for the home team. And no matter how many times I watched the Pirates and the Steelers lose, there was always that hope that this time they were going to win, and, if I played ball hard enough and well enough, I'd be out there with them some day.

Chapter 4

My reward for finishing my education at Humboldt grade school in five years was an invitation to serve as one of the honorary ushers for South High's commencement at Carnegie Music Hall. The commencement took place in 1950 on a warm June evening, but there was a Cold War chill in the air. Just four months earlier, Senator Joseph McCarthy had delivered his infamous Red Scare speech in Wheeling, West Virginia, just seventy miles down the road from Pittsburgh. Red-baiting McCarthy claimed he had a list of 205 workers in the State Department who "were known to the Secretary of State as being members of the Communist Party," but he would have been hard-pressed to find a subversive on the stage, in the audience, or among the handful of nervous honorary ushers at South High's graduation ceremonies.

The commencement had all the patriotic zeal required by McCarthy and his lunatic fringe to face the dangers of the Cold War. After the traditional Salute to the Flag and the singing of "The Star-Spangled Banner," the top four seniors, apparently inspired by the lyrics of "America the Beautiful," gave patriotic speeches on America's "Spacious Skies," its "Pilgrim Feet," its "Heroes Proved," and its "Patriot's Dream." Once the school chorus sang "The Battle Hymn of the Republic," Principal Chester Sterling handed out the awards and diplomas. Before the graduating class bravely marched out into the 1950s, they recited "The American's Creed" and joined the chorus and their parents in singing "America."

As I stood in the back of the auditorium, after directing proud working-class parents to their seats, and picked up a copy of South High's 1950 yearbook, I couldn't help but notice the symbol of the atom embossed on the maroon cover. Inside, the title page featured a drawing of an ideal middle-class family, a well-dressed father and mother, their daughter in pigtails and their son in a sailor's cap, gazing up at the middle page of a larger-than-life book, titled *Turn of the Century*. All around them were dancing images of things past and things to come in transportation, engineering, science, medicine, and entertainment. The end page of the yearbook had a drawing of a high school senior gazing up at a V-2 rocket headed for destination unknown, though in 1950, it could have been Moscow as well as the moon.

While commencement speakers droned on, I spent most of my time thumbing through the gallery of photographs that a year later would include my own seventh grade class. I also glanced at the message in the yearbook to the 1950 graduates from principal Sterling who warned South High's mid-century graduates that they would soon have to decide "whether or not science is to heal or destroy." He feared that the current generation of graduates, faced with the destructive power of the atom and hydrogen bombs, would lack the courage and determination to overcome the dangers facing them.

My own encounter with the country's political paranoia came about a year later when *I Was a Communist for the FBI* appeared at our local Arcade Theater. The movie, which was actually filmed in Pittsburgh and had scenes shot on the South Side, was about a steelworker who pretends to be a Communist sympathizer to help the FBI infiltrate a Red-tainted labor union. Mr. Hopkins, my junior high social studies teacher, was much more concerned about the teacher in the movie who gets into trouble because she fails to see the dangers of Communism. I didn't know that a teacher in the Pittsburgh public school system had just been fired because of her past ties with the Communist Party, but Mr. Hopkins, with his mild-mannered Clark Kent appearance barely concealing his paranoid disposition, knew about it and the danger that the firing had for his own job.

Mr. Hopkins, unhappy with the class clowns who pretended they were blind and on fire during air-raid drills, thought our parents should take us to see *I Was a Communist for the FBI*. It was a good warning for our generation about the threat of Communism and the likelihood of an A-bomb attack, especially on Pittsburgh with all its steel mills. He told us he was going to set a perfect example for us on how to be "good Americans," even if it meant paddling patriotism into our "thick hides." I felt a bit nervous about Mr. Hopkins's scare tactics, but the wooden paddle hanging on a nail just above his desk seemed much more of a physical threat to my seventh-grade health than any Communist conspiracy or Russian A-bomb.

South High, with or without the help of Mr. Hopkins's warning to his junior high students, seemed to be doing its part in making sure that its students didn't contribute to the downfall of America. With the opening in 1940 of South Vocational across the street from the original dirt-brick high school building, South High, one of Pittsburgh's first secondary schools when it opened in 1898, was the only school in Pittsburgh's public school system at that time to offer both academic programs and vocational training.

By 1950, South High's students were taking either a full complement of academic courses—though, coming from working-class families, most of us weren't going anywhere academically—or a wide range of shop courses, including Bake, Shoe Repair, Cosmetology, and Sewing. America may have been on the brink of an atomic war at the beginning of the 1950s, but South Voc students were being trained to make sure that Pittsburghers were well-fed, well-heeled, and properly groomed while waiting anxiously for the Russians to drop the bomb.

South High's crowning glory going into the 1950s, however, was still on the drawing board. At the same time as television was heralding the birth of a golden age in American sports, construction was beginning on a new athletic field, just across the street from the high school annex. By 1951, South High Stadium, with its grassless, rock-hard field, was ready to host not only the Orioles home football games but also the City League championship game, the annual rivalry between North Catholic and Central Catholic, and the charity game played each year between North Catholic and Boys Town.

The stadium was to become the centerpiece for Pittsburgh's high school sports in the 1950s, but it would also become a magnet for racial trouble. When one of the city's segregated high schools played on its field—and powerhouse Westinghouse, from Pittsburgh's Homewood area, was always in the City League's championship game in the 1950s—fistfights often erupted in the stands. After the game, it was not unusual, especially if Westinghouse won, for whites to harass and chase Westinghouse students over the Tenth Street Bridge and back to their black ghettos.

The appearance of mounted policeman at the City League's championship football games was a blunt, visible sign that there was more than the threat of Communist collaborators and mushroom clouds hanging over the South High's next generation of students as we headed down Carson Street each weekday morning in the early 1950s. America's racial segregation and class imbalance were also clearly on display.

Our students were mostly white and working class and, with few exceptions, more likely to become butchers, bakers, and cabinetmakers or marry a butcher, baker, or cabinetmaker, than to become college graduates and community leaders. A few male and fewer female students had aspirations to attend Pitt, Duquesne, or Carnegie Tech and become doctors, lawyers, or engineers. Most males, however, wanted to be mechanics or machinists, if they weren't going into military service, while most females saw themselves becoming secretaries, beauticians, or, as they wrote in the yearbook, "just making someone a good wife someday."

There was a strong ethnic character to South High students, though the ethnic mix was diluted by the South Side's Catholic high schools— Lithuanian St. Casimir's, Polish St. Adalbert's, and German St. Michael's. There were enough O'Hara's, Tambellini's, and Schultz's to suggest a melting pot, but the dominant ethnicity at the school was upper Carson Street Serbian—every other name seemed to be Topich, Marovich, or Stepanovich. Not so visible were black students, the "coloreds." There were well over one thousand students attending South High in each year during the early 1950s, but there were no more than fifty African Americans, and often far less, in any given year. Except for the handful of students who trickled into South High from the few black families still living on the South Side, the lower-class black children of Pittsburgh lived and went to school across the river in segregated enclaves on the Hill and in Homewood.

When I started the seventh grade at South High in 1950, I was eleven years old and entering my own small world of changes at a time when the city and the country were going through dramatic transformations. Instead of walking the few blocks home from Humboldt at lunchtime,

I now had to eat in the basement school cafeteria where I passed up the lunch special, usually a tasteless, overcooked spaghetti or an odd-tasting, pinkish-looking stew, for something that look a little safer. I'd used my three eight-cent tickets to buy two orders of mashed potatoes and stuffing, served in scoops, and a plate of buns, and my two seven-cent tickets for cartons of chocolate milk. It wasn't the healthiest lunch, no daily requirement of the four basic food groups, but it certainly did the job. It filled us up for the rest of the day and made an afternoon nap in class far more inviting than making life difficult for our teachers.

After school at Humboldt, I'd been a good boy, running to butcher shops and grocery stores to buy things for supper. I'd also routinely picked up my mother's waitress uniforms at Gerson's cleaners, my father's white shirts at the Chinese laundry, and the afternoon papers at Ross's before heading home. But now I started hanging out after school in the booths at George's and Lipori's, where I played the jukebox and the pinball machine. I listened to unfit girls tell dirty jokes, and became nervous when the only openly "queer" played Doris Day's "Secret Love" over and over again. While Kay Starr spun love's wheel of fortune, Tony Bennett crooned about love's riches, and Johnny Ray wailed about its heartbreak, I listened, with hormones raging and acne erupting, to a dark-haired, overripe girl named Sandy tell her favorite joke about the farmer and his three daughters, all married on the same day. "That night," at least according to Sandy, "the farmer passed by their bedrooms and heard the first daughter cryin', the second daughter laughin', but he didn't hear no sound at all coming from the third daughter's bedroom." "The next morning," Sandy wickedly concluded, "when the farmer questioned his three daughters, the first said she was cryin' 'cause it hurt, the second said she was laughin' cause it tickled, but the third said there was no sound 'cause she was taught never to speak with her mouth full." When we asked Sandy what she would do on her wedding night, she gave us her best Mona Lisa smile and didn't say a word.

At the high school, with the halls and stairs filled with girls as old as seventeen and eighteen, the art of stairwell bumping, perfected in grade school, now had a definite feel of reality to it. In my junior high classes, however, there wasn't much to get excited about except for Annette and her amazing high-riding breasts. We took class sightings every day and argued fiercely about them in the cafeteria because her breasts always seemed to be pointing in different directions. Most of us refused to believe the worst, but a few cynics, noting the shifting latitude and longitude under Annette's sweater, darkly claimed there was more Kleenex than Annette inside her bra. As for Annette, she may have been fodder for our juvenile fantasies and money in the bank for Hugh Hefner, but she was also fated to marry right out of high school. At our ten-year high school reunion in 1966, when someone else got the award for having the most kids, Annette yelled out, "You can have it, honey!"

When I wasn't gazing at Annette's mysterious otherness, I was struggling to pay attention in classes that were preparing me for college, though neither of my parents had made it past the ninth grade. My impressive IQ test scores and two double promotions in grade school were enough to convince my teachers and principal that I was college material, but as far I was concerned Pitt's towering Cathedral of Learning, visible from the South Side, might as well have been on the moon, rather than just across the river. For the next six years, I sat in English classes, where an array of mean-spirited battle-axes, including my senior-year nemesis Miss Wilkinson, demanded we read *Ivanhoe, A Tale of Two Cities,* and memorize Shakespeare soliloquies, though I was more likely to read *Classics Illustrated* for my book reports and discover a switchblade before me rather than a dagger.

I did see the Hollywood versions of *Ivanhoe* and *Julius Caesar* when they came to a Downtown movie house because city school kids usually got free passes for a weekend matinee when some filmed classic rolled into town. Watching jousting tournaments and castles being stormed was always fun, and a dark, seductive Elizabeth Taylor brought raven-haired Rebecca to life for us far better than Sir Walter Scott's prose. But it was a little hard not to moan and howl at the sight of Marlon Brando in a toga just after he and his motorcycle gang had terrorized small-town America. When Brando shouted out, "friends, Romans, countrymen" some bored high school kid in the audience yelled out, "lend me your bike."

I also attended ever-advancing math classes with their spiraling and unending axioms and logarithms and memorized conjugations and long passages of Roman history in four years of Latin. Added to all this, if you were a "college-bound" male student at South High, were classes in Mechanical Drawing because going to college in Pittsburgh in the 1950s meant you were going to be an engineer. Female students went off to Home Economic classes to prepare for the domestic life that was their likely fate, even if a few of them dared to dream of college. But males were being taught to letter properly and copy designs for bridges, factories, and suburban homes by a mean-spirited Mr. McCall, who knew most of his students would end up working in mills, rather than designing them. He also knew I was so nervous that I had trouble drawing a straight line, and deliberately hovered over me at every opportunity to ridicule my handiwork. He'd take my feeble attempt at copying a blueprint, raise it high above his head, and laughingly ask the class if they wanted to see what a blueprint looked like "if you held it in front of a fun house mirror."

Sitting in classes that were demeaning and completely removed from the realities of my working-class life on the South Side, however, was the least of my worries in high school. While I reluctantly memorized Shakespeare and Latin and copied out formulas and blueprints, I also had to survive a gauntlet of shop, gym, and health classes run by male teachers who seemed to take great pleasure in inflicting punishment and pain on our adolescent bodies. The basement of South High was made up of little shops of horror, where saws buzzed, vises clamped, and aproned teachers roamed about, looking for the chance to show off their well-designed paddles on the mechanically challenged. It was also where coaches, forced to teach health classes, took out their frustrations and sometimes their hangovers by throwing erasers at talkers or clamping their death grips on the shoulder blade of any student who fell asleep during a movie—and we saw lots of old Army movies about venereal diseases in our health classes. After watching those movies, we believed that maybe our mothers were right after all—our "dicks" were going to rot and fall off if we weren't careful about sex.

South High's gym and pool were also located in the basement, though gym classes weren't so bad. Once in a while a coach would get ambitious or feel guilty about our physical condition and drag out the medicine balls, but most of the time they let us choose up sides and play basketball in the winter or walk a few blocks in the spring to Armstrong playground to play softball with pick-ax handles for bats. What most of us dreaded was the weekly plunge into South's indoor pool, especially during the winter months. It's one thing to risk smashing or losing a finger in shop, but having your testicles frozen and your penis shrunk by ice-cold pool water was a male adolescent's worst nightmare. But once a week we stripped down in the locker room, took a cold shower, soaked our feet in a tray of disinfectant, and then eased or flung our naked bodies into water so frigid it appeared to have a coating of ice floating on the surface.

The only consolation was that the pool was located near my shop classes, so all I had to do was borrow the hall pass and, on my way to the boy's room, peek at the girls through a crack in the door of the indoor pool. Though I knew the girls wore bathing suits and I was so nervous at getting caught that I never saw much of anything, I'd brag to my lunchroom pals that Annette's breasts were definitely real and a sight to behold as she emerged out of the icy water in her wet, clinging swimsuit.

As much as I hated my junior high ordeals of floating naked in an icy pool, risking fingers in wood shop, and suffering physical abuse in health class, they were nothing compared to the horror that waited for me every day in my homeroom on the third floor of the oldest section of the high school. I started seventh grade about the same time as the arrival of Frederick Schmidt, the new music teacher and a former student at South High. Flamboyant and ambitious, red-faced and wild-haired, Mr. Schmidt returned to his old school with great expectations. He wrote a new fight song—our old one sounded suspiciously like "On Wisconsin"—and a new alma mater that cast a "golden glow" on our aging high school and the soot-covered South Side.

Mr. Schmidt had a great passion for music and a violent temper to go with it. If someone in the band wasn't paying attention or was horsing around, he'd explode in a rage, shout out the offender's name as if he had just issued a death warrant, and, like an angry Zeus, hurl a music stand in the direction of the unlucky drummer or tuba player. Fortunately, Mr. Schmidt wasn't much of an athlete, and the stand usually fell far short of its target and the rest of the scrambling band. In his calmer moments, he loved singing at assemblies—usually it was something from Sigmund Romberg or Jerome Kern—but his greatest joy, when he wasn't bellowing out his need for "stout-hearted men," was starting up the first marching band in South High history to perform on the new football field. When I arrived at South High in the fall of 1950, I was one of thirty confused, unlucky, and mostly untalented seventh graders assigned to Mr. Schmidt's band homeroom and I stayed there for six embarrassing years.

I don't know how we were selected for South High's first band. I blamed those damn IQ tests I took at Humboldt and my double promotions for my own bad luck, but we were such a hodgepodge of South High's best and brightest and its worst and dimmest that random selection was a more likely factor. So far as I was concerned, I hated the band and thought playing a musical instrument was something an accordion player did at a Polish wedding or on the Wilkins Amateur Hour. I wanted to play baseball and football and perform heroic feats on the dirt and dust of South's new stadium, not form a giant S on its playing surface.

When Mr. Schmidt assigned instruments, I don't know what cruel twist of his blazing temperament was at work, but in a roomful of future trumpet and trombone, clarinet and saxophone, bell and drum players, he decided I should play the E-flat alto horn, the poor cousin to the rich baritone horn and the elegant French horn. In a high school marching band, the E-flat horn is the dwarfish brother and the musical counterpoint to the tuba. While everyone else plays the march, the tuba hits the downbeat, the "oomph," and the E-flat hits the upbeat, the "pah." At a time in my life when I was already feeling like a misfit because I was younger and smaller than everyone else, I was not only stuck in the band but also consigned to the musical world of the offbeat.

But the embarrassment of learning musical scales and proper fingering, of playing "Twinkle, Twinkle Little Star" over and over again in front of my disbelieving, working-class parents, was just the beginning, just a prelude to the approaching horror of being an original member of South High's band. It was bad enough when my alcoholic father mockingly said I was driving him to drink with that "goddam horn," but the real nightmare began when Mr. Schmidt thought we were ready to take the field as the marching Orioles. Until then we were safely tucked away on the third floor, a distant and irritating sound to the rest of the school, as we learned to play our instruments. But now we were out on the football field, kicking up dust, sounding off like the GIs in *Battleground,* and desperately trying to learn our left foot from our right, and how to make an S that didn't look like a deformed snake.

As badly as we performed, we looked even worse. Mr. Schmidt, who had little funding to work with, came up with a makeshift uniform of white baker's pants, courtesy of South Voc, a white shirt and black tie, reluctantly paid for by our parents, black evening capes, bought wholesale from God-knows-what costume shop, and black military furlough caps trimmed in orange, ordered out of an Army and Navy store catalog. We looked absolutely ridiculous—a bizarre, Halloween mixture of the vocational, the operatic, and the military. Our own student body mercifully ignored us as we marched onto the field, went into a cryptic formation, and tooted out what sounded vaguely like our new fight song and alma mater. But when we marched across the field to murder the other school's fight song, we were met with a barrage of flying missiles. At one game we had to restrain Tony Loriso when a well-thrown apple core came sailing into the mouth of his tuba.

As awful as we looked and played, we were the perfect marching band for a football team that rarely won a game and was humiliated each year by Westinghouse and its powerful single wing. It took a rarity, a terrific South High varsity team, to give us the proper stage to expose ourselves as the worst-looking band of musical misfits in the history of western Pennsylvania high schools. Our band mercifully never played at varsity basketball games, but all that changed in my junior year when South High, led by four black players in the starting lineup, won the 1955 City League basketball championship and went on to meet the McKeesport Tigers for the Western Regional title and a chance to play in the Pennsylvania state final. Just when I thought we were safe for the year, except for the humiliation of a spring school concert and faking my way through the "Dragnet" theme, a glowing Mr. Schmidt announced to his incredulous band that we had been invited, along with McKeesport's band, to play at a sold-out Pitt Field House.

When we arrived at the game in our military caps and opera capes, we looked like an oddly dressed band of field house vendors. But we made it through the crowd without having anything thrown at us and found our seats in a reserved section just behind one of the backboards. After we played our school's new fight song—"fight for dear old South High let's fight / fight with all your might"—to a smattering of applause,

South High band, 1954. A gloomy Peterson third from left, first row.

and for once no booing, we settled in to watch what we thought was going to be a terrific basketball game. But all we had to do was look across the Pitt Field House to realize we were about to experience the worst humiliation of our band years.

While our thirty-piece band sat insecurely in its capes, we stared across at a huge, gaping section of empty seats, three times the size of our own section of bleachers. After a few minutes, we heard the beat, beat, beat of bass drums, then the blaring sound of the opening bars of "Hold That Tiger" as the 100-piece McKeesport band came roaring through the crowd. Colorful, loud, and in tune, they were everything that a high school band should be, as they dazzled the crowd and sunk us into a fit of despondency. Even the unsinkable Mr. Schmidt seemed overwhelmed by the wave of sound that engulfed us.

Unfortunately, McKeesport's basketball team added to the nightmare by defeating our Orioles that night. Not content, however, to win the game, they also tried to bully and humiliate our players. For the next two hours, the all-white McKeesport team tormented our starting black players, calling them "blackbirds" and "Sambos." They also taunted our only white player on the court by calling him a "white nigger." And, after every time-out and at the end of every quarter, the McKeesport band added to our misery, drowning out our feeble efforts to play our fight song by blasting "Hold That Tiger" again and again through the rafters of the Pitt Field House.

I had no idea that my growing unhappiness and frustration in high school were part of a teenage angst that was registering itself, however distortedly, in the books and films of the 1950s. As I dragged myself and my E-flat horn down the hill from the Pitt Field House to the rented bus taking us back to the South Side, I'd yet to read *The Catcher in the Rye* and, when I first heard the title years later, thought it was a baseball novel. I did see *Rebel Without a Cause,* but I didn't pay much attention to James Dean or his movies until he became an instant cult figure after dying in a car crash. Caught up in my own problems in high school, it would take years for me to realize that whiny, misunderstood rich kids were defining my working-class, teenage years for generations to come.

From our inner-city perspective, the teenage punks in *Blackboard Jungle* and the motorcycle gangs in *The Wild One* were far more appealing and entertaining. Few of us could afford black leather jackets and motorcycle boots, and we had better sense, even if we were teenagers, than to rebel against a South Side patriarchy of hard-drinking steel workers, grease monkeys, and truck drivers. But we were quite capable of terrorizing an inexperienced female teacher in the same way we were being bullied and abused by our shop teachers and coaches.

In the ninth grade, we drove Miss Brown, our new English teacher, out of the classroom and into a new career. Blonde, attractive, and sincere, she wanted to make a difference, but it wasn't going to happen in our class. She was a perfect target for everything from the leering taunts of her male students to erasers hurled at her back by jealous females. One afternoon, after a student shouted out that the aging grammar books she'd just passed out "smelled like shit," she burst into tears and called us "nothing but a bunch of hoods and whores." She stormed out of the classroom and never looked back.

By the time we were in senior high, there were as many bad boy waves and duck asses as there were military crew cuts in our class-rooms, and our speech, already mangled by our "Souseside" dialect, was riddled with a variety of crude and cruel obscenities, though "mother-fuckin' cock-sucker" seemed at the top of the list. But rivalries, unlike those in Hollywood teenage movies, were settled in the halls with fistfights, not with switchblades and zip guns, and were quickly broken up by the hall patrol and our teachers. Every once in a while somebody did bring a switchblade to school, but mostly to show off; and we weren't above making life miserable for Duquesne Light by shooting out streetlights with a BB gun. But the only knife fights and chicken runs I saw were in the movies, and the only cut I suffered was on one of my knuckles in the shape a tooth when one of my buddies tried to get even a few weeks after I'd crushed his thumb with one of my cleated heels in a game of leap frog. After we were dragged into the principal's office, we were more concerned about detention or suspension than any animosity toward each other.

Of course, while Hollywood was misrepresenting and sensational-izing teen life in the 1950s, at least as we were living it on the South Side, it also gave us some badly needed fantasies and diversions. When Cinerama wasn't hurling us down roller-coaster dips, we had spears and tomahawks thrown at us from the 3-D movie screen. But the plots of those 3-D movies were truly awful, and Cinerama mostly gave us glorified travelogues. Far more satisfying was the steady diet of mutated insects, blood-sucking "things" from outer-space, and amphibians lurking in caves, tunnels, and black lagoons that fed our Cold War paranoia.

The only real success for Hollywood in the early 1950s, at least as far as we were concerned, was CinemaScope and stereophonic sound because they made the movies bigger and louder. CinemaScope didn't rescue the movies from Milton Berle, Arthur Godfrey, and studio wrestling, but it was perfect for an insecure generation of male adolescents leering at a make-believe generation of Hollywood blonde bombshells and foreign sex kittens. There was nothing more inspiring of teenage wet dreams and masturbation than larger-than-life Marilyn Monroe and Monroe copycats like Jayne Mansfield and Mamie Van Doren bouncing across the CinemaScope screen or more mesmerizing than Kim Novak in a low-cut pink dress as she oozed across the dance floor in *Picnic*. Most of us saw the movie several times and would have given our souls to trade places with bad boy William Holden.

While Kim Novak, with that throaty voice and bedroom eyes, was replacing the girl next door and tomboys of my prepubescent fantasy world, I was still painfully shy in approaching girls. When I made the mistake of going to a junior hop, one of my buddies convinced his sister to dance with me, but, no William Holden, I shook so violently we had to stop long before Eddie Fisher could finish singing about his papa and why he was so wonderful. Afterward she told everyone I was "a sweet kid," but she was afraid I was "gonna turn into butter" before she got me off the dance floor.

With most of the girls in my classes either ignoring me or treating me like their kid brother, my emotional and physical outlet was playing baseball and dreaming of playing some day for the Pirates. My sexual fantasies haunted me and drove me to distraction and embarrassment, but baseball was my heart's desire. As I struggled through the 1950s and my high school years, my goal was to play varsity baseball for South High on my way to the big leagues. Shakespeare and Latin, trigonometry and mechanical drawing, Mr. Hopkins and Mr. McCall could all go to hell. I looked out at Pitt's Cathedral of Learning as I came down the hill from playing ball at Quarry Field, but, in my mind's eye, Forbes Field, not much more than a baseball's throw away from Pitt, was my destination. I had no interest in college and no intention of taking the advice of my teachers, who kept urging me to do more before it was too late.

My buddies and I played baseball every day, beginning in the cold, soggy spring, through the dog days of summer, until the chilly fall rains turned our fields of dreams into mud. With neighborhood rivalries and individual pride at stake, we played a punishing, reckless brand of baseball that often went beyond a love of the game itself. I don't remember a single score from the hundreds of games I played on South Side's dirt fields, but I do remember the jammed fingers, the charley horses, and raspberry thighs and how fiercely we fought to win and how bitterly we took our losses. I lived for those games and couldn't imagine what I would do with my life if I didn't play some day for the Pirates.

In the late summer of 1954, just a few months after I'd turned fifteen, my dream of playing baseball in the big leagues was all but shattered by a freak change in the weather. The day should have been warm and sunny in Pittsburgh, a perfect day to play baseball or sit in the left-field bleachers or the right-field grandstand at Forbes Field. But it was a rare August day, rainy and just cool enough to hint at the fall and football season. So somebody dug up an old football, and we headed up to Ormsby playground for a game. We should have had enough sense to play touch football, but the field was soft and muddy and we decided to play tackle. More than anyone, I should have had better sense because I'd broken my left elbow ten years earlier after being pushed off a wall by Joey Chisel, and the elbow had never been set properly.

The only play I remember from the game was taking the snap from center and rolling out around right end. I turned the corner and headed up field until Davy Tuschak, who had the build of a middle linebacker, threw a rolling block into my legs. As I flew into the air, I made the mistake of reaching out with my left arm to cushion my fall. When all the weight of my body came down on my left hand, my elbow, weakened by an earlier break, snapped in two like a twig.

I must have been in shock because I can't remember any pain as I sat there and stared in disbelief at my dangling arm. And I have no memory of seeing the bone sticking through my skin, though I had a compound fracture of the elbow. But the flow of adrenaline got me to my feet and helped me walk the two blocks up to St. Joseph's emergency room, while a couple of my football buddies, after I pleaded with them "to go get my mom, for chrissake," ran down to Merriman Way.

I remember how heartsick I felt, just sitting there on the hospital cot, moaning "I'm sorry" again and again to my poor mother, who had enough to worry about without all this happening—and my relief when the emergency room doctor reset my arm and made it look normal again except for the bloody puncture wound. I was ready to go home, but the doctor, after examining the area around my elbow and feeling something loose, told my mother I'd have to stay in the hospital until a specialist had a chance to look at me. My mother and I thought he meant overnight, but I ended up having a pin inserted into my elbow and had to stay in the hospital for a week of recuperation, bad hospital food and great-looking nurses who added a whole new dimension to my sexual fantasies by flirting with me.

Once out of the hospital, I still had to spend every Saturday morning for the next several months in the clutches of bald-headed and liver-spotted Dr. Kerr, a famed Pittsburgh specialist who had operated on my elbow. Every Saturday morning, my mother and I walked up to St. Joseph's, where Dr. Kerr, who seemed as ancient as the Pittsburgh hills, examined my scarred elbow and yelled at me for being just lazy and not working hard enough to straighten out my arm. With a grip all out of proportion to his frail appearance, he'd yanked my arm back and forth until I nearly passed out from pain.

But, no matter how many times Kerr yanked my arm, no matter how many times I carried a bucket of bricks up and down Merriman Way, my arm never completely straightened out. Dr. Kerr's handiwork, as I went back to school to pursue my badly damaged dream of playing big-league baseball, was a permanently crooked arm with only a 70 percent radius. I would never again be able to touch my left shoulder with my left hand, and my elbow, with its ugly six-inch scar, would stick out at an angle for the rest of my life.

As my playground scars and high school hang-ups seemed to increase alarmingly, my life at home continued at its own usual, if dismal, pace. My mother still worked the graveyard shift at Rodgers Dairy, waiting tables and slicing lunchmeat, and tried, without much success, to make the best of a bad situation at home. My father kept drifting in and out of gas station jobs and making things worse with his drunken binges. The only difference was that I was growing up and becoming more aware of my parents' emotional alienation.

All through my grade school years I'd always looked forward to payday, when there was a payday. Every Friday after school, my mother, my sister, and I waited for my father to come home from work so we could go out to supper at the Arcade Café. But by high school I'd grown tired of waiting and watching my mother get upset on the Fridays my father didn't make it home, of walking up to Carson Street and standing outside while my mother searched for my father in every beer joint from Bianchini's to Kotula's. When she finally gave up, we ended up by ourselves in the Arcade Café.

I'd also had my fill of looking across the table at my mother on the verge of tears, of watching our waitress, Sophie, with her bleached-blonde hair, caked-on make-up, and bloated face, walk over with our glasses of water and ask, "Where's the old man?" I hated it when Sophie told my mother, "I ain't met a man yet worth cryin' over" and that she was going to bring over a hot cup of tea "just to cheer Lil up." And I was no longer comforted when my mother said, "Don't let Sophie bug you 'cause her life ain't no bed of roses. There's lots worse than your dad out there, and Sophie knows all about it."

In my high school years, I also discovered that my father wasn't as paranoid as I thought he was about my mother fooling around. His name was Harold Friedman, but we called him Ben. With his pug nose and thick black hair, he reminded me of Billy Conn, the light heavyweight champion, who, like Ben, had grown up in Pittsburgh's tough East Liberty district. Like Conn, Ben always seemed to be getting into scraps, but he wasn't much of a fighter for someone who had what my mother called "that goddam Jew boy's chip on his shoulder."

Ben had served in the navy during World War II and had been aboard one of the ships during the atomic bomb testing in the Pacific. Afterward he'd been stationed at Guantanamo Bay and was the reason my mother had those Cuban dolls hidden in the attic. After he came out of the service, he tried several jobs, but finally settled on becoming a policeman. When I first met him, he was driving a patrol car in the Hill District, which was a dangerous assignment, especially for someone who believed that the Hill's black residences were no better than animals.

My mother met Ben at Rodgers, where he'd hang out at night and wait for her to finish work. I was too emotionally immature to think of Ben as my mother's boyfriend and too alienated from my father to feel that my mother was doing something wrong. All I knew was that sometimes my mother would gather up my younger sister, Nancy, and me and make some excuse to my father about visiting her sisters a few blocks down on 17th Street. When we walked around the corner to Wharton Street, Ben would be waiting in his bathtub-shaped 1949 Mercury, the one made famous by James Dean in *Rebel Without a Cause*. I was always glad to see Ben and looked forward to riding in his car.

Most of the time, we'd drive out to the newly opened Greater Pittsburgh Airport to watch the planes take off and land. Afterward we'd stop off at the Original Hot Dog in East Liberty for what Ben said were the best-tasting hot dogs in town. A few hours later, when we were back on Wharton, my mother would warn us not to say anything to my father about Ben because it would spoil everything. Nancy and I didn't understand why we had to keep Ben a secret. We were just glad that he liked our mother well enough to treat us to a ride because we didn't own a car. But we made the promise to my mother because she looked so serious and never did say a word to our father because we didn't want the rides to end. We also felt a strong emotional bond with our mother and felt no such loyalty to our father, who always seemed to be ruining things for us.

Our outings with Ben were also the only occasions when my sister and I had fun together. I was more than five years older and didn't have much use for Nancy. Blonde, blue-eyed, and sweetly innocent, she loved and trusted her big brother, but I mostly resented and ignored her. As far as I was concerned Nancy was taking up physical and emotional space in an already claustrophobic working-class world. She was just another mouth to feed and body to clothe in a family on the daily edge of financial disaster because of out father's drinking.

Nancy was simply in the way, an alien presence inside with her dolls and cutouts and an annoying tag-along when my buddies and I played out our adventures around the alley's scrap yard and rag factory. Worse yet, she was someone I had to entertain outside when my parents had "things" they needed to talk about, their code, I later suspected, for having sex. At best, she was a tackling dummy for my football fantasies and an easy target for snowballs. During the great

Thanksgiving blizzard of 1950, my mother was furious when she discovered I forced Nancy to lie down in a snow bank, while I tried to bury her like an Egyptian mummy. My mother angrily reminded me that they were using Army tanks as snowplows, but the idea of Nancy being run over by a tank was even better than the thought of waiting for her buried body to be discovered during a spring thaw.

My problem, besides my resentment of my sister, was that I never realized how strong my mother's emotional bond was with Nancy and how deeply Nancy was affected by my father's failure to show her any expression of love. Completely self-absorbed with my own problems at South High, I also had no idea how Nancy must have been bothered by her Humboldt teachers, who expected her to live up to her Whiz Kid brother and his double promotions. As the years went by, Nancy was becoming an emotional time bomb, and, by her teenage years, was ready to explode with anger and revenge.

Other than our secret rides with Ben, our only other outing was the annual Seventeenth Ward picnic at Kennywood Park, but by my high school years even that was fading out. While my mother and her two sisters still packed baskets and stayed in one of the picnic shelters, my father and uncles no longer bothered coming out to the park. If any male turned up, it was usually Ben, who would conveniently meet us at the merry-go-round in the evening and offer us a ride home.

Instead of going out to the park with my mother and aunts, I now took the special school bus out to Kennywood with Butch, my cousin and fellow band member, so we could be there when the swimming pool opened and get our first serious sunburn of the year. Afterward, if we were lucky, we'd bump into girls from the band and ride everything from Kennywood's famous roller coasters to the rocket planes that slowly soared out over the lagoon. I remember spending one glorious afternoon with flute-playing Mary Alice as we rode the Jack Rabbit with its breathtaking double dip, the Racer with its wild turns that brought me as close to a female body as I would ever get in high school, and the Pippin with its giant dips and its dark tunnel that invited a bold move beyond my timidity.

If I hadn't been so immature and insecure, Mary Alice would have been the perfect girl for me. In junior high, besides being a fellow sufferer in the band, she was a cute, short-haired tomboy who loved to play sports. By senior high, she had the firm body of an athlete and was attractive and popular enough to rise above the stigma of the band and become head cheerleader. She was also smart enough to be in the National Honor Society and so outgoing that the same boys who didn't take much notice of Mary Alice in junior high were eager to spend time with her.

Mary Alice was also the inspiration for my high school fantasy, my own version of *The Stratton Story*. A shattered elbow wasn't quite the same as an amputated leg, but, like a game Jimmy Stewart, I'd struggle to overcome my handicap, learn to play baseball again, and make the varsity team on my way to the big leagues. Mary Alice, my outgoing, cheerleading June Allyson, would quit dating football players, inspire me in my comeback, and marry me at Forbes Field's home plate as the announcer intones "Dick Peterson stands as an inspiration to all of us, as living proof of what a man can do if he has the courage and determination to refuse to admit defeat."

All Mary Alice and I needed to live happily ever after high school was to teach our kids the joy of playing sports, the risks of double promotions, and the value of rolling with a punch, or, in my case, a hard tackle. But popular Mary Alice had her world of dances, committees, and dates in high school, and I couldn't dance, wasn't very popular, and was afraid to ask a girl out. But I did have baseball, the one thing I thought I was truly good at. So, bad elbow or no bad elbow, Mary Alice or no Mary Alice, I took my glove and spikes over to South High's stadium in the spring of my junior year and, still possessed by the burning hope of playing in the big leagues some day, tried out for the varsity baseball team. My chances of making South High's varsity team as a sixteen-year-old junior were not that great because there were so many returning seniors, and, thanks again to my double promotions, I was two years younger than most of them. But, for once, a few things broke my way, including the weather.

It was so cold and rainy that spring in Pittsburgh that for weeks we couldn't go onto the muddy field. So we bundled up, lobbed the ball around on the track, played a little pepper, and ran sprints and laps. When I began to outrun bigger and stronger athletes, I caught the eye of Coach Cue, which wasn't easy because after he'd had a steel plate placed in his head, the result of a flung baseball bat fracturing his skull, he didn't

South High baseball team, 1955. Peterson kneeling, fifth from left.

seem to notice much of anything. When the spring rains stopped long enough for the field to dry out, Coach Cue told his returning seniors to pick out their uniforms and had the team captain tell "what's-his-name, you know, the little, skinny kid with the crew cut " to pick through the leavings to see if there was something that would fit.

My next break actually started out as another high school humiliation because the only baseball pants that fit had a large patch on the seat. I could roll up the sleeves of my oversize baseball shirt and tighten my belt to keep my pants up, but I couldn't hide that damn patch. As far as the seniors were concerned, I was just some raggedy-ass kid running around in the outfield. But every time I went after a line drive in the gap, Coach Cue could see the patch on my ass as I ran down the ball and made the catch.

After I'd proven in drills and on the field that I could run and catch, the real challenge came in batting practice where, as a right-hand hitter, I had to expose my left elbow to a thrown baseball. When I stepped into the batter's box, the scar on my elbow looked like an arrow pointing to the mound, taunting the batting practice pitcher to hit me. My personal torturer, Dr. Kerr, had also warned me that if I broke my elbow again, I'd end up with a withered arm. But I dug in at the plate, choked up on the bat, concentrated on the pitcher's hand, and managed to foul off pitch after pitch until a tailing, inside fastball glanced off my chin. My third break, and it was the charm, came when the batting-practice pitcher, who was now afraid he was going to kill me, lobbed the next pitch up to the plate. When I lined it over the pitcher's head, Coach Cue came laughing into the batting cage, called me "Petey" (the first time anyone had called me by my father's nickname), and told me I wouldn't play that much, but I was on the team.

Chapter 5

In the spring of 1955, at the same time that as I was trying out for South High's varsity baseball team and dreaming of becoming a big-league ballplayer, the Pirates were breaking in a flashy rookie outfielder from Puerto Rico. Barely sixteen, I had to hustle and fight for a spot on my high school team, but Roberto Clemente, the Pirates' twenty-year-old rookie, didn't have to worry all that much about making Pittsburgh's major-league roster. The Pirates had drafted him from the Brooklyn Dodgers' farm system and, under the "bonus-baby" rules of organized baseball, would have to return him to the Dodgers if they didn't keep him in the major leagues for the next two years.

Most kids who dream of playing in the big leagues grow up worshipping a baseball hero. Early on, when our fathers take us out to our first games, our hero usually becomes the home team's superstar, a Babe Ruth, Joe DiMaggio, Mickey Mantle, or, in my case, a Ralph Kiner. Later, when we start to play the game ourselves, our hero-worshipping becomes more practical. When I became a pitcher in the Little League, my loyalty shifted from the Ruthian Kiner to a crafty Murry Dickson. I wasn't that big and didn't throw very hard, so the undersized, rubber-armed Dickson was a perfect Little League model for my big-league aspirations. By the time I was ready to try out for my high school team, I was an outfielder and needed a new hero, someone with the speed and daring to cover the spaciousness of Forbes Field, defy its brick walls, and inspire me to make my high school baseball team.

It should have been a match made in baseball heaven. After watching an assortment of incompetent outfielders on a Pirates team that had finished in last place for the past three years, I was ready for the real thing, an outfielder who could actually play the outfield without misjudging fly balls. All the reports coming out of spring training claimed that the new Pirates rookie outfielder was a natural. He had that rare thing for a Pirates ballplayer in the early 1950s, the athletic ability and instincts to play the game. Pittsburgh sportswriters described his arm as a "rifle," his speed as "electrifying," and his base hits as "frozen ropes." He was still a green rookie, but he was exciting to watch even when he was making mistakes. Al Abrams, the longtime baseball beat writer for the *Pittsburgh Post-Gazette,* wrote, "Every time we looked up there was Roberto showing his flashing heels and gleaming white teeth to the loud screams of the bleacher fans."

By 1955, attending Pirate home openers had become a spring ritual for me and rare fun for Pittsburgh's long-suffering baseball fans who always had to wait until next year. Though the Pirates had finished in the second division eight of the last ten years, they were great in home openers, winning ten straight going back to 1945. I had the good fortune, for a young baseball fan in the 1950s, of being born in mid-April or about the time major-league teams used to play their home openers. Every year, once I started junior high, I took my birthday money, killed off my grandmother so I could get away with playing hooky, and rode the streetcar or hitchhiked out to Forbes Field to watch the Pirates open the season. But in 1955, I didn't go to the home opener and, in my mind, cost the Pirates their home winning streak when they lost to the Phillies. I had high school baseball practice that day and was afraid that if I missed practice, I'd be cut from the team.

I tried to redeem myself for jinxing the Pirates' home-opener winning streak by going out to Forbes Field three days later for a Sunday doubleheader with the Dodgers. Along with the other 20,499 fans, I witnessed the debut of Roberto Clemente, who had sat out the first three games of the season, and the beginning of one of the most provocative and fabled careers in the history of baseball. In the bottom of the first inning, we watched Clemente, batting third in the lineup against lefty Johnny Podres, scratch a single off Pee Wee Reese's glove for his first major-league hit. Podres would go on to win the final game of the 1955 World Series against the Yankees. Moments later, we cheered as Clemente wheeled around the bases and scored his first major-league run and the Pirates' first run of the game on a triple by hometown hero Frank Thomas. When Thomas scored on Reese's error, it looked like the Pirates were on their way to winning their first game of the season and getting me off the hook for abandoning them in their home opener.

Because of Clemente's debut, that first game of the Sunday double-header has taken on great significance in baseball history. But for Pirates fans who were at the game, there was nothing memorable about watching the Dodgers come back and trounced the Pirates 10–3. The Dodgers also went on to win the second game 3–2, despite two more hits by the rookie Clemente. Walking out of Forbes Field that Sunday, we were much more concerned about the Pirates opening the season with a five-game losing streak (it would eventually reach eight before they finally won their first game) and the probability that, with or without Clemente in the lineup, our woeful team was headed for its fourth straight season in the National League cellar.

My memories of Clemente's first season with the Pirates are fragmentary, but consistent with the mostly negative and hostile attitude of Pittsburgh fans toward minority ballplayers in the 1950s. Despite the presence of Branch Rickey in the front office since 1951, the Pirates, well aware of their white working-class fan base, had been very slow to sign minorities. Among Clemente's teammates in 1955 was second baseman Curt Roberts, who, as a rookie in 1954, was the first African American to play in a Pirates uniform, seven years after Jackie Robinson's history-making rookie season with the Dodgers. After an outstanding season with the minor-league Denver Bears, Rickey had signed Roberts to a major-league contract, after warning him that he would face the same abuse directed at Jackie Robinson: "Since you are the first black Pittsburgh Pirate, you are going to go through these things. You can't let your temper flare up."

Roberts didn't encounter the ferocity of abuse directed at Robinson, but he still had to endure racial taunts from Pirates fans and the unwillingness of his white teammates to have anything to do with him. Years later, Roberts's widow said that their house "was always full in Denver, white and black, Cubans, Panamanians. . . . Everybody came to our house. But there were *never* any white players invited to my house in Pittsburgh. That tells me that Curtis wasn't treated very well." The effect on Roberts of fan hostility and teammate indifference was devastating. After an outstanding season in Denver, he pushed himself too hard and slumped badly in his first year with the Pirates. He was still in the starting lineup when the Pirates opened the 1955 season, but Gene Freese started at second base when Clemente made his major league debut three games later. After appearing in only six games in 1955, Roberts was sent to the minor leagues. He played briefly for the Pirates in 1956 before he was shipped back to the minors and never played in a major-league game again.

As I watched the Pirates in 1955, I couldn't understand why the Pirates had spent good money on the likes of Roberto Clemente. I may have been looking for a new baseball hero, but Clemente was certainly not the answer to my prayers. Clemente was just another oddity on a team that was the laughingstock of the National League. He had an awkward head-bobbing, knees-pumping way of running the bases, and a nonchalant way of catching fly balls at thigh level that seemed a poor imitation of Willie Mays's famous basket catch. Clemente also had a way of digging his back foot into the far corner of the batter's box in a way that suggested he was afraid of getting hit by a pitch.

My youthful skepticism about Clemente's worth to the Pirates, however, had deeper roots than his erratic fielding and mediocre hitting. In Clemente's rookie season, I was growing up in a working-class world defined by its ethnic enclaves, its steel-mill mentality, and its deep hatred and fear of minorities. The very geography of Pittsburgh seemed to cry out for racial segregation. The working-class North Side and South Side formed white-populated barriers along the banks of the Allegheny and Monongahela, in effect isolating much of the black population of Pittsburgh between the rivers. There were plenty of bridges crossing the Allegheny and Monongahela, but they were avenues for commerce, not for integration.

My racial attitudes while growing up in Pittsburgh were pure South Side. When I started attending Pirates games with my father in 1948, a year after Robinson broke through organized baseball's racial barrier, we avoided Dodgers games in the early part of the season because of the "goddam niggers" from the Hill and Homewood who were "ruinin' things" for Pittsburgh's white fans by coming out to Forbes Field to see Robinson play. The pre-Rickey Pirates were a good draw early in 1948 because they were contending for the National League pennant, but when Robinson and the Dodgers came to town the ballpark was always packed and, to the dismay and resentment of many of Pittsburgh's white baseball fans, fully integrated.

Despite my father's belief that the Dodgers and Jackie Robinson were destroying baseball, we did go out to Forbes Field for a Pirates-Dodgers Sunday doubleheader because of the pennant race that summer. I don't recall the details of the games or even Robinson's presence on the playing field, but I do remember the crowd. Because so many people wanted into the ballpark, the outfield was roped off to allow for the overflow attendance. As exciting as it was to walk on the warning track and outfield grass with my father, to be on the same playing surface with Ralph Kiner, Wally Westlake, and ex-Dodger Dixie Walker, my most vivid memory remains the encounter with so many black fans and my father's disgust at baseball's great experiment. When one unhappy white fan looked down at me and asked my father if "your kid thinks he's at the zoo with all the goddam apes walkin' round,'" we thought his remark was pretty funny and right on target.

Oddly enough in 1948 my parents and I were living in a house on Merriman Way, one of the last vestiges of Pittsburgh's black population on the working-class South Side. In his preface to *Fences*, a play about a former Negro League ballplayer set in Pittsburgh's Hill District, August Wilson notes that "the destitute of Europe" were welcomed participants in the industrial growth of Northern U.S. cities, but not "the descendants of African slaves," who migrated from the South: "The city rejected them and they fled and settled along the riverbanks and under bridges in shallow, ramshackle houses made of sticks and tar-paper." Merriman Way was a racial anachronism in 1948 where white families lived on one half of the block and black families on the other half, though neither race was happy with or trusted the other.

By 1955, the black families were gone from Merriman Way, their rented houses now abandoned and eventually demolished. The black kids from the alley were, no doubt, high school students at Fifth Avenue or Westinghouse in the city's racially segregated areas—if they hadn't already dropped out of school. But I had no more concern for their lives across the river than I had for Clemente's struggles while playing baseball in a city with fixed racial barriers and attitudes. While Clemente was enduring his teammates' slurs and snubs and racial taunts

78

from the stands, I was playing ball on the South Side's segregated ball fields. Taught to resent and mistrust blacks, there was no way I could even begin to grasp the incredible difficulties facing Latin American ballplayers like Clemente, who, while they struggled against both racial and language barriers, were being treated as if they were "double niggers," as Clemente himself later phrased it, because of their skin and their heritage.

Thanks to the sports sections of Pittsburgh's three daily newspapers, the *Post-Gazette,* the *Sun-Telegraph,* and the *Press,* I was aware of Clemente's heritage, but only because Pittsburgh sportswriters exaggerated and made fun of his accent in their stories and columns. The quotations attributed to Clemente on the occasions when he played well often made him sound ignorant and stupid. The irony was that working-class Pittsburghers themselves have a notoriously odd way of talking because of our habit of dropping syllables and clipping endings from words. We also have a curious way of inventing odd sounding words, like "et" for eaten or "gumbans" for rubber bands, when the proper word took too much of an effort to pronounce or didn't suit us. Add the most common profanity that sprinkled the vocabulary of a working-class Pittsburgh youth of the 1950s and you were ready for a typical "Souseside" conversation, usually one that began with someone asking, "Man, yunz goin' to the fuckin' knot hole game or what d'yunz wanna fuckin'do?"

But Clemente's way of speaking, as exploited by Pittsburgh sportswriters, was an entirely different matter because his accent was foreign. If Clemente had a good day it was because he "heet the peetch gut." If he started the season slowly, as he usually did, it was because he "no run fast and no play gut" until the weather got "veree hot." In one of the first interviews to appear in a Pittsburgh paper, Les Biederman, baseball beat writer for the *Pittsburgh Press,* in reporting from spring training in 1955, gave his readers this example of Clemente's "broken English." When Biederman asked him, "Did he have a girlfriend," Clemente supposedly responded: "No, me no married yet. Not even girl. I still young. Plenty time. I make big ligues first. One theeng I like Merica, new autos. Buy myself new auto. Whee!" When Biederman asked Clemente to name the best player he'd ever seen, Clemente answered, "Best player ever see Weelie Mays. Ah! Weelie play center field. I play left Puerto Rico. When young boy see Josh Geebson play Puerto Rico. Great heetair. Zoom."

Not content with using phonics to make Clemente sound ridiculous, Pittsburgh sports writers, exploiting Clemente's flamboyant and erratic play, also portrayed him as a "Puerto Rican hot dog." When he slammed his helmet to the ground after striking out, he was too "hot headed." If Clemente accused pitchers of throwing at him or missed a game because of an injury, he was a "pop-off" or too "lazy" and full of himself. When he complained about his chronic back problem, the result of an automobile accident in Puerto Rico during the winter before his rookie season, sportswriters accused him of being a whining hypochondriac. If he had the flu or diarrhea, tonsillitis or chipped bones in his elbow, the common perception was that Clemente wasn't playing because he was too moody and only interested in looking out for "numero uno."

If Clemente's rookie season in 1955 had been similar to Jackie Robinson's remarkable first season, things might have been different in Pittsburgh. Robinson led Brooklyn to the national pennant in 1947, its first since 1941, and was named National League Rookie of the Year. Clemente, despite his athleticism, struggled at the plate and fielded erratically, while the Pirates, after their eight-game losing streak to open the season, stumbled to a 60 and 94 record and a last place finish for the fourth straight year. Of course, Robinson, a veteran of the Negro Leagues, was twenty-eight in his rookie season, while Clemente, in just his second year in professional baseball, was only twenty-one years old. But tolerance and understanding, except for its losing teams, were not the trademarks of Pittsburgh's baseball fans in the 1950s, and I was your typical Pirates fan.

Another of the many ironies of Clemente's early career with the Pirates is that the National League Rookie of the Year in Clemente's rookie season would become Clemente's teammate the following year. Bill Virdon, traded by the Cardinals to the Pirates in May 1956, was, in my eyes, the perfect center fielder—and he was white. He wasn't flashy and didn't have terrific speed, but he always seemed to get a great jump on the ball. He ran effortlessly in the outfield and was courageous in challenging the brick walls at Forbes Field. Fundamentally sound, he always caught the ball at eye level and never seemed to throw to the wrong base. It also helped, at least for a skinny and insecure high school outfielder from the South Side, that Virdon wore glasses and was more of a slap hitter than a slugger. His nickname during his career in Pittsburgh was "the Quail" because his bloop hits into the outfield looked like dying quails.

Playing next to Virdon in the outfield, Clemente came to life in 1956. The Pirates, instead of starting the season with another losing streak, actually generated some early season excitement when first baseman Dale Long, whose only notoriety had come from Branch Rickey's failed experiment in 1951 to convert him into a left-handed catcher, homered in eight consecutive games, something never done before in baseball history. The Pirates, to the astonishment of Pittsburgh's long-suffering fans, were still in the pennant race in June. We cheered at our senior prom when the bandleader announced another Pittsburgh victory, the only good news that evening for my date—but, by season's end, despite Dale Long's heroics and the great seasons of Clemente and Virdon, the Pirates had fallen into seventh place where they finished again in 1957.

While Clemente played erratically in his early years and developed a reputation for showboating and whining, the Pirates were acquiring players, like Virdon, who actually knew how to play baseball, and, in 1960, won the National League pennant and the World Series. But, if Clemente felt racially isolated when he came to Pittsburgh in 1955, he could take little comfort from the racial makeup of the 1960 World Championship team. It was the perfect ball club, with the exception of Roberto Clemente, for a city still defined by the ethnic and racial attitudes of its mill-town population.

Pirates fans had plenty of white heroes to choose from in 1960. We had the fiery, ex-Marine Don Hoak at third, the Duke All-American Dick Groat at shortstop, the Polish Bill Mazeroski at second, and the flaky Dick Stuart at first. With Clemente in the outfield were Bob Skinner, who'd drawn exaggerated comparisons to Ted Williams from Pittsburgh sportswriters, and my baseball idol Bill Virdon, who seemed to play center field so flawlessly. Clutch-hitting Hal Smith and roly-poly Smoky Burgess were the catchers for a pitching staff led by Mormon Vernon Law, Mississippian Vinegar Bend Mizell, Purdue graduate Bob Friend, and local favorite Roy Face, who worked as a carpenter in the off-season. Barely noticeable on the World Series roster were African Americans Joe Christopher, used mostly as a pinch-runner, and an aging

Gene Baker, who came from the Negro Leagues with Ernie Banks, but was now reduced to a pinch hitter and utility infielder.

For Clemente, 1960 was the turning point in his career. He had a wonderful year, the best yet in his career. After his most successful season in the major leagues, Clemente also experienced his "biggest thrill" when Bill Mazeroski's home run in the bottom of the ninth gave the Pirates a dramatic, improbable victory in the World Series over the heavily favored New York Yankees of Mantle, Maris, and Berra. Pittsburgh, denied a world championship since 1925, erupted with unrestrained joy and danced its way into a Mardi Gras frenzy. Hundreds of thousands of Pittsburghers, known more for their hard-nosed attitudes and tough mindedness, embraced each other into the small hours of the morning. Returning to Puerto Rico, Clemente had good reason to believe, though he didn't participate in the celebration, that he had finally won the acceptance of teammates, sportswriters, and fans. In the afterglow of the World Series victory, he believed his nightmare in Pittsburgh finally was over.

Less than two months later, however, Clemente's personal happiness turned bitter when his teammate Dick Groat was named the National League Most Valuable Player. Groat, who sat out the last month of the season with a broken wrist, had won the National League batting title with a .325 average, but Clemente, playing in 144 games to Groat's 122, hit .314, led the team in runs batted in, and was second on the Pirates in runs scored. When he found out that Don Hoak, another white teammate, had finished second in the balloting, and Clemente himself had finished eighth, he felt his "double nigger" heritage and not his talent and accomplishment had determined the vote. Because of the insult to his pride, Clemente refused to wear his 1960 World Championship ring. He also carried his resentment and bitterness into the next season and seasons to come and played baseball as if it were a form of punishment for those who had slighted him and injured his pride and spirit.

After winning the World Series in 1960, the Pirates failed to win another championship for the rest of the decade. A bitter Clemente, however, played like a champion and had a Hall of Fame decade in the 1960s. Angered at not getting the recognition and credit he felt he deserved, he played brilliantly in 1961, winning his first National League batting title and earning his first Gold Glove award. By the end of the decade, Clemente had won four batting titles, nine Gold Glove awards, and in 1966, though the Pirates failed to win the pennant after contending all season, was finally named the National League's Most Valuable Player.

Slow to integrate in the 1950s, the Pirates finally began changing the racial makeup of their team in the 1960s by bringing in more African American and Latin American ballplayers. Clemente, finally attracting national attention for his brilliant play and encouraged by the presence of more minorities in the clubhouse, began speaking out against racial prejudice and became one of baseball's most controversial figures.

Clemente believed Latin American ballplayers were a minority within a minority, treated in the 1960s the way African Americans had been treated in the 1950s. He stated publicly that Latin Americans were commonly dismissed by the press and some of their own teammates as being too temperamental, lazy, and even gutless in clutch situations. With his success, Clemente now felt a responsibility to do something for black athletes, both African Americans and Latin Americans. By speaking out in the clubhouse and playing inspired baseball, he became a team leader and role model for younger players like future Hall of Famer Willie Stargell. In a decade characterized by political turmoil and racial change, Clemente became the most visible and provocative sports figure in Pittsburgh.

While the integrated Pirates of the 1960s were a reflection of the social changes brought about by the Civil Rights movement of the decade, there were Pittsburgh fans inclined to see the presence of so many black athletes on the Pirates as the reason for the team's failure to repeat the success of the 1960 season. The Pirates were plagued in the early 1960s by key injuries and terrible trades, but the team's struggles on the field and its declining attendance were often linked to the Pirates' growing number of black athletes, despite the brilliant play of Clemente and strong seasons from Willie Stargell, Donn Clendenon, and Bob Veale. The most provocative event of the decade in Pittsburgh was the appearance in 1967 of an all-black Pirates lineup with the exception of its white starting pitcher. The event was the historical culmination of

Clemente (#21) and Stargell (#8), 1965 (courtesy of the Pittsburgh Pirates)

Jackie Robinson's integration of major league baseball ten years earlier, but there were Pirates fans who preferred to see it as a good reason for staying away from Forbes Field.

The best reason for going out to the ballpark in the 1960s for Pittsburgh's color-blind fans was the performance of Roberto Clemente. He attracted more and more attention as one of the game's most exciting performers and at the end of the 1966 season, after nearly leading the Pirates to the National League pennant, edged out Dodger pitcher Sandy Koufax for the Most Valuable Player award. The *Sporting News* also named him National League Player of the Year. As the first Latin American to win the combined awards, Clemente became a national hero in Puerto Rico and validation for the island's youth that Latin Americans could achieve greatness and respect in America's game.

Unfortunately, Clemente, despite his superstar status, was still plagued by controversy in Pittsburgh because of his running feud with Pittsburgh sportswriters, whom he blamed for his long struggle for national recognition. During the 1960s, Pittsburgh sportswriters regularly reported on Clemente's strained relationship with popular manager Danny Murtaugh, seized upon and often exaggerated Clemente's complaints about his lack of recognition, and mocked his frequent ailments and his refusal to play with injuries. When Al Abrams wrote a story in the *Post-Gazette* based on hearsay, claiming Clemente had asked the Pirates to trade him because he wasn't appreciated in Pittsburgh, Clemente refused to talk to Abrams for over a year. Shortly after Clemente's death, Abrams claimed he now wanted to write a book about Clemente because "he had great compassion for his fellow human beings. I saw that part of him early, long before he was killed in an airplane crash on a mercy mission." Abrams added, however, that Clemente "also had the human frailties. He was outspoken. If something bothered him, he never let it ride. And he had to be number one in everything."

I'd like to remember that, unlike Pittsburgh sportswriters, my awareness of Clemente's significance in baseball history increased in the turbulent decade of the 1960s, but it didn't happen that way because I never connected the country's political and racial turmoil with my life as a baseball fan. Proud of Clemente's four batting titles, I didn't think there was anything wrong with Pirates broadcaster Bob Prince calling Clemente "Bob" or "Bobby" or shouting "Arriba, Arriba" when

Clemente batted in clutch situations. I enjoyed watching Clemente's aggressive base running, his daring catches, and his breathtaking throws from right field, but I also believed, like most sportswriters and fans, that Clemente was dogging it when he sat out games with his mysterious ailments. When Clemente won the National League's Most Valuable Player award, I didn't connect it with his pain at not getting the award in 1960 and had no idea of the emotional impact of the honor on Puerto Ricans and its historical importance to Latin American ballplayers.

When Martin Luther King was assassinated in 1968, I ignored, as did most Pittsburgh fans, Clemente's pivotal role in the Pirates' refusal to play its season opener in Houston and in the team's eloquent public statement that the Pirates, who had eleven black players—more than any other team in the major leagues at the time—were acting out of respect for "what Dr. King has done for mankind." Clemente, who had met the Reverend King a few years earlier, was deeply disturbed by the death of the civil rights leader and troubled by the conduct of Pirates officials in the aftermath of the assassination: "When Martin Luther King died, they come and ask the Negro players if we should play. I say, 'if you have to ask Negro players, then we do not have a great country.'"

Though I was growing up in Pittsburgh when Clemente began his major league career in 1955 and followed Pirates fortunes throughout the 1950s and 1960s, I didn't really begin to appreciate Clemente's true greatness until the beginning of the 1970s and the last few years of his life. In 1970, the Pirates provided a new stage for Clemente's brilliant play when they moved from a decaying Forbes Field to Three Rivers Stadium. A few weeks later, the ball club finally honored Clemente with a special fan appreciation night.

Thousands of Pittsburgh fans, joined by hundreds of Puerto Ricans, including Clemente's parents, showered him with gifts, but we also learned something about Clemente's compassion when he asked that the event also be used to raise money for the Pittsburgh Children's Hospital. That season the Pirates and Clemente went on to their first Eastern Division championship, but were swept by the Cincinnati Reds in the National League playoffs. In 1971 they repeated as Eastern Division champions, beat the San Francisco Giants and Willie Mays in the playoffs for the National League pennant, and played in the World Series for the first time since 1960 against a powerful Baltimore Orioles team that had swept the Oakland A's for its third straight American League pennant.

Roberto Clemente's performance in the 1971 World Series is the stuff of baseball legends. For the record, Clemente fielded brilliantly, batted .414, homered in the seventh and deciding game, won 2–1 by the Pirates, and was the overwhelming choice for the Most Valuable Player award. But the 1971 World Series will always be remembered as Clemente's personal showcase. After watching his dazzling performance, Roger Angell, writing for *The New Yorker*, claimed that Clemente had played "a kind of baseball that none of us had ever seen before—throwing and running and hitting at something close to a level of perfection, playing to win but also playing the game almost as if it were a form of punishment for everyone else on the field."

In the Pirates clubhouse after the World Series, Clemente displayed the same pride, grace, and dignity millions had seen on the playing field. When congratulated by Pirates broadcaster Bob Prince, Clemente looked directly at the television cameras and, speaking in Spanish, addressed his parents, *"En el dia mas grande de mi via, les pido sus bendiciones"* ("On this, the proudest day of my life, I ask for your blessing"). Facing sportswriters, who now came to praise Clemente after years of accusing him of being a showboat, a malcontent, and a malingerer, Clemente asked, not for their blessing, but for vindication. After seventeen years he'd finally proven his greatness to the baseball world: "Now people in the whole world know the way I play."

In the weeks after the World Series, he used his public appearances to support Curt Flood's court case against baseball's reserve clause. He also criticized major league baseball for failing to hire black managers. Claiming that his World Series triumph had given him a chance "to help lots of people," he announced plans to build a Sports City in Puerto Rico for children, so they would have the same opportunity to use sports to better their lives.

For the Pirates, the 1972 season, with the exception of Clemente's 3,000 Major League hit in his last at bat of the season, was bitterly disappointing. After repeating as Eastern Division champions, they lost a heartbreaking fifth and deciding game to the Cincinnati Reds in the National League playoffs. Of course, the worst was yet to come for the Pirates and for the rest of the baseball world. Less than three months later, on December 31 at 9:22 P.M., a DC-7 cargo plane filled with supplies for the victims of a devastating earthquake in Managua crashed into the Atlantic minutes after takeoff, killing everyone on board, including Roberto Clemente, who had personally taken charge of the relief efforts in Puerto Rico to help Nicaragua's recovery.

Clemente's tragic death, so terrible and shocking at the time, has since become a part of baseball's fabled history. Like Lou Gehrig, Clemente has become an icon of the perfect athlete cut down by death at the height of his glory, frozen forever in time and now immortalized as one of baseball's greatest stars. In 1972, Clemente became the first Latin American to enter Cooperstown, when the Baseball Writers Association of America, after waiving the mandatory five-year waiting period, elected Clemente to the Hall of Fame. His statue now stands outside the right-field gate of PNC Park, where Pirates fans, after walking across the Clemente Bridge, can pay their homage before entering the ballpark. His plans for a Sports City in Puerto Rico have, thanks to his widow Vera Clemente, become a reality, and, in 1998, on the twenty-fifth anniversary of his induction, the Hall of Fame opened its first bilingual exhibit in honor of "The Great One."

My own understanding of Clemente's greatness has also changed since his death, but my memories of growing up with Clemente have tempered my understanding. I've read numerous tributes from fans and writers, but I know that most of them form a revisionist narrative of Clemente's life and career. Throughout his early years in Pittsburgh, because he was dark-skinned and Puerto Rican, he struggled in an unfriendly and hostile environment. Even when he began to play brilliantly, he remained a controversial figure because he was often branded with negative traits that were nothing more than sportswriters' exploitation of the stereotype of the Latin American ballplayer. To prove his worthiness and greatness, Clemente had to capture, at the age of thirty-seven, the national spotlight of a World Series, and, to become a hero and the stuff of legend, he had to die tragically in the humanitarian effort to help the victims of a terrible earthquake.

Roberto Clemente's photograph, taken by a friend of mine during Pirates batting practice in 1972, now hangs in my study as a tribute to

Clemente and as a reminder of what I didn't see and didn't know when I watched Clemente early in his career. Growing up with Clemente, I had no understanding or sympathy for what he was going through because I shared the racial attitudes and feelings that made his career and life so difficult and miserable. Over fifty years after first watching Clemente play at Forbes Field, I feel a sense of loss every time I look at the photograph, but my feelings are as much for the Clemente of my youth as for the Clemente cut down in his greatness and now glorified by biographers and historians.

The Clemente I see in the 1972 photograph is a ballplayer confident and secure in his greatness. In my mind's eye, however, I also see an image of Clemente in 1955, proud of his ability as a ballplayer and his heritage as a Latin American, yet emotionally estranged from America's national game because of his race and ethnicity. No wonder that on the proudest day of his life and at the very moment that the baseball world was honoring his greatness as a ballplayer, he remembered his love of baseball and family as the source of his emotional strength and asked his parents, and not the press or his fans, for their blessing.

Chapter

Making South High's baseball team in my junior year was my happiest moment in high school, but, as it turned out, it was also the worst thing that could have happened to me. Short, skinny and, at sixteen, the youngest player on the team, I didn't get into many games that spring, and, when I did, it was mostly as a pinch runner or for late-inning defense in the outfield. My only moment of glory came when I made a lunging catch of a line drive in short right field and excitedly threw to first base to double up the runner. Fortunately, our first baseman, Willie Strothers, was also the center on the basketball team because he had to make a leaping catch of my adrenaline-laced throw.

It wasn't much of a debut, but it was more than enough to convince me, despite my crooked elbow, that playing baseball was what I'd be doing for the rest of my life. When I left South High in 1955 for summer vacation, my guidance counselor, Mr. Moore, warned me to start thinking harder about hitting the books and earning a scholarship to college, but my own plans were for hitting baseballs and signing with the Pirates. I spent the summer going out to Forbes Field and watching rookie Roberto Clemente and his teammates bungle their way into last place. Encouraged by their incompetence, I spent long hours practicing on the South Side's ball fields. In those pre-steroid days, I also stuffed myself with banana splits and drank milk shakes to put on weight and prayed at night for a miraculous growth spurt.

I'd been preparing myself to play for the Pirates as far back as I could remember. At the start, when I was probably eight or nine years old, I'd thrown a black-taped baseball that resembled a lump of coal back and forth with my father or my uncle Tony. When I couldn't find anyone interested in playing catch, I threw a rubber ball against the low wall across from my grandparents' house and, in my best imitation of Rosey Rowswell and his colorful baseball language, broadcast imaginary Pirates games, which the Pirates always won. Everyday my poor grandmother, who had enough trouble understanding English, heard me shout, "there goes a doozey-marooney" or "that's the old dipsy-doodle" and worried that I was losing my mind. When she heard a loud thud against the front of the house, followed by her grandson yelling out Rowswell's joyful celebration of a Pirates home run—"get upstairs and raise the window Aunt Minnie, here she comes"—she wondered who this poor, mysterious Aunt Minnie was and why "she never made it."

When my grandmother heard too many thuds against the house and feared she was about to suffer Aunt Minnie's fate of a broken window, she begged me to "go play ball" somewhere else. I loved my grandmother almost as much as the Pirates, so I'd take an old pick-ax handle from one of my grandfather's junk piles, sling it over my shoulder, and march down the alley to the railroad tracks, where I'd load up my pockets with the stone nuggets hugging the rails. I'd head to the riverbank and, once there, drive stone after stone into the river with the pick-ax handle. When my hands started to blister, I'd hunt out discarded wine and beer bottles, hurl them into the river, and use the rest of the stones to sink the bottles as they floated by on the river's current.

No memory of playing an actual game of baseball stands out in my mind's eye until my Merriman Way buddies and I started to venture around the corner to Ormsby playground on the weekends when there were no adult softball league games cluttering up the ball field. Ormsby's all-dirt, pebble-laced field was perfect for a gang of ten- and eleven-year-olds because it had the dimensions of a slightly lopsided Little League field. On weekends, Ormsby became our baseball Eden where, with no adults around, we taught ourselves to play the national pastime with all the innocence and enthusiasm of novitiates. We were working-class Adams, delighting in the physical joy of playing ball. We chose up sides, played every position, and began to dream that the entrance to the Brady Street Bridge, catty-corner to the ball field, would some day be the heavenly passage to playing for the Pirates out at Forbes Field.

My first strong memory of playing ball at Ormsby, however, suggests I had something more inside me than a simple delight in playing baseball. We didn't have umpires for our games, so we usually argued whether a ball was fair or foul or a runner was safe or out until one side or the other gave in and the game went on. I can still see the ball I hit bouncing fair over the third-base bag before it rolled into foul territory and remember running, to the shouts of "foul ball, foul ball," until I made to second base. When the other side kept arguing that the ball was foul and refused to go on with the game, I became so upset that I took my taped bat—the only bat we had that day—and, to the yells of "crybaby," and "quitter," stormed off the field and ran back down the alley.

It was my bad temper more than a bad call that was the serpent in our baseball Eden. I was the same child, now several years older, who threw a fit when he lost at musical chairs and had to be dragged out of the bingo hall. It's also possible that I was now smart enough—I was the kid with two double promotions in grade school—to realize a simple economic truth about baseball—if you owned the equipment you controlled the game, and I was the one with the bat. More likely, once we began competing against each other, I was learning that winning was becoming a part of my love for the game and a source of pride. In our working-class world there weren't many reasons to be feel good about ourselves, but playing well and winning games on the ball fields of our youth gave us our first feelings of self-worth.

My ball-playing buddies and I were fortunate, at least for a short while, that we weren't disturbed in our play by a lurking adult world, but all that changed when the Little League first came to the South Side in 1951. At the age of twelve, I finally had my first encounter with organized baseball and adult coaching. I loved playing baseball, but my season in the South Side Little League taught me that humiliation is also possible on the ball field. Little League didn't ruin my desire to play the game or my dream of playing for the Pirates, but what it taught me about prejudice and ridicule fit perfectly with the life lessons I was gathering on the working-class South Side.

When I brought my birth certificate and my big-league dreams to the Little League's spring sign-up meeting at Lithuanian Hall, all I wanted was a chance to pitch because my father had been a pitcher in his green years on the South Side. But a few weeks later, at our first practice, our coaches divided us into four groups—the Bucs, the Cards, the Cubs, and the Reds—and, ignoring our pleas, assigned us to positions. The biggest kids with the strongest arms were now Little League pitchers, even though some of them couldn't hit the side of a warehouse. The bulkiest kids, ridiculed in school as "tubbies" and "lard asses," were handed catching gear because they now had value as human backstops. The sons and nephews of coaches were the lucky ones, the privileged class, and were assigned to play the coveted infield positions. The rest of us, the leavings, had to scramble for a position in the outfield.

At our first practice, I chased after fly balls with the mob of kids running around in the outfield until I was finally called in to take a turn at bat. When I got to home plate, one of the coaches told me to "hustle it up, kid, 'cause it's gettin' late." After I'd taken three hopeless swings at pitches not even close to home plate, he laughed and told me to go with the rest of the "strike-out kings" to the far end of the field, where I was assigned with the other rejects to the Bucs' minor league team.

Being a minor leaguer was a major embarrassment because the big-league Bucs wore brand-new uniforms and rubber-cleated shoes and played on a perfectly measured and fenced-off section of Quarry Field, an adult-sized baseball field located just up the hill from Ormsby's playground. Minor leaguers were handed T-shirts with the Little League insignia on the front, had to wear their own "tennies" and played on a badly chalked-off area in the far right-field corner, where we wouldn't interfere with the major league games. We also had to go through the further embarrassment of wearing our T-shirts, as others proudly marched in their uniforms, in a parade down Carson Street to celebrate the inaugural year of South Side's Little League. I hated that T-shirt and had to be dragged by my mother to the parade. She told me, "it ain't gonna kill you, so put the goddam thing on and let's go."

The T-shirt didn't kill me because my minor league career was mercifully short-lived. I got my break in a warm-up game of catch with one of the few coaches who seemed to know something about baseball. Rubbers, who got his nickname from the rubbers he stood on in his sandlot days as a pitcher and his uncanny resemblance to Plastic Man, told the other coaches "yunz need to take a look at this kid."

Rubbers had noticed my tendency, as a right-hander, to throw almost from the side and to sling my wrist and arm away from my body as I delivered the ball, a habit I'd picked up in games of catch with my submarine-throwing father. Because of my unorthodox delivery, the ball, without my realizing it, was curving inwardly to Rubbers on every throw. According to Rubbers, a pitcher, if he wants to curve the ball, will snap his wrist across body. When he does, the ball will break down and away. But my ball, because of the way I threw, had a natural bend to it. Put me on the rubber, claimed Rubbers, and my pitches would bend and sink into a right-handed hitter rather than curve away from him.

Rubbers laughingly identified what I was throwing as a "Little League screwball" and told the amazed assembly of red-eyed, beer-bellied coaches that "little Dickie here's a goddam natural, a right-handed Hubbell, and he don't even know it." To my delight, I was moved up to the majors and pitched the rest of the summer for the Bucs.

I'll always be grateful to Rubbers for rescuing me from the minors, but I wasn't the second coming of Hall-of-Famer Carl Hubbell. My screwball wasn't much more than a modest inshoot that started to drop when the law of gravity took over because I couldn't throw very hard. But whatever Rubbers wanted to call it, my inshoot fooled enough batters for me to win a few games and helped the Bucs into the playoffs. My only problem with pitching in the Little League majors was that I still had to wear my minor-league T-shirt when I went to the mound against the nicely uniformed Cards, Cubs, and Reds, because all the Buc uniforms had been handed out. I was pitching in the majors and wearing my brand-new rubber cleats, but I still suffered from the indignity of looking like a minor leaguer every time I went out to the mound.

It wasn't until the season was nearly over and our starting shortstop quit the team that I finally got my Little League uniform, though I wasn't so sure his uniform was the one I wanted to wear. Roy, our shortstop, had the misfortune of being hit by pitched balls so many times, including twice in one game, that he had trouble staying in the batter's box. We wore a flimsy plastic-flap boxing headgear in those pre-helmet days, but poor Roy probably felt he needed a suit of armor against our league's wild pitchers. His real problem, though, was that there was no coach with enough sense in his head to tell Roy there was nothing wrong with a young kid being afraid of a hard ball coming right at him. In those days we were told by adult coaches to "hang in there". . . . "be an Oriole". . . . and "take one for the team." If we got hit with a pitch, we were told to "rub it off" and hustle down to first

Now pitching for the Little League Bucs, 1951.

base because we didn't want the pitcher to think we were "yellow." When poor Roy started to buckle his knees at the plate on every pitch, our coaches ridiculed him until Roy quit the team in tears.

When the Bucs made it to the championship game, I was on the rubber, wearing Roy's unlucky uniform and throwing my rinky-dink inshoot against the Cubs and their tall, hard-throwing ace, who would in a few years become an all-city quarterback. As I stared in at my catcher's sign, though it didn't matter how many chubby fingers he put down because I had only one pitch, I should have realized that Roy's uniform was a jinx. I can't recall much about the game or even the final score, but I do remember giving up lots of runs, getting hit with a pitch—the uniform must have been a magnet for baseballs— and losing a lopsided game. I'd begun my Little League career as a disgruntled minor-league discard and ended it as the sobbing losing pitcher in the championship game of the Little League's first season on the South Side.

My father, who started coming up to Quarry Field to watch our games once he found out I was pitching, came over to our bench after the championship game was over. As I cried in misery, he said that what I was going through was just a part of baseball. Losing the game was tough but "hey, it ain't the end of the world, you know." If I wanted to cry "hell, that's okay, just go ahead and bawl." He'd bet Honus Wagner and Pie Traynor "cried plenty" when they lost tough games.

My father tried to say all the right things, but I wasn't buying any of it. I hated losing so much I didn't give a damn if I ever played baseball again. Instead of shaking hands with the Cubs players and accepting my runner-up trophy like a good sport, I stormed past everyone and headed out through the exit gate in the far right-field corner, After a few hours of wandering along the river bank, destroying every living plant in sight, and shattering every abandoned bottle that I could find, I discovered even sore losers get hungry. When I got home, my father was nowhere in sight, but my runner-up trophy was waiting for me on the kitchen table. I looked at my mother, but she just shrugged and said, "Your old man thought you still might want this thing once you quit your goddam poutin'."

Thanks to my father, I kept my trophy, though my Little League experience made me leery of adult coaches and even more of a hot-tempered loser. The South Side had no Pony League or American Legion ball, so at least I didn't have to worry about adult supervision again until I started playing on tournament teams at Ormsby playground. During the 1950s, Pittsburgh's City Parks ran four tournaments each year in slow-pitch softball, touch football, basketball, and volleyball. There was also an annual games day tournament, held each spring in the South Side Market House, where, if you were good enough or sometimes just willing to walk the ten blocks down Carson Street to represent Ormsby, you could compete in anything from checkers to Ping-Pong.

The competition was so poor in chess—I was playing matches against poorly educated, inner-city kids—that I won a gold medal, actually a gold-painted lead medal small enough to balance on the tip of my index finger. Playing chess was an oddity—it was something I'd picked up in high school study hall from a band buddy—in a teenage working-class world more suited to playing card games for comic books, flipping baseball cards, and rolling dice on baseball and football game boards. More common for my playground buddies was competing in

Ormsby's silver medalists in volleyball. Peterson kneeling, second from the left, 1958.

the city's team tournaments. We played well enough to bring Ormsby the miniature gold—the team sports medal was bigger than the games medal, but still small enough to cradle in the palm of your hand—in touch football, basketball, and softball, and a silver in volleyball. Making tumbling catches and getting clutch hits in winning the gold medal in softball also restored my confidence in my ball-playing abilities after my Little League meltdown.

When we played in the city tournaments, our coaches were Ormsby's park directors, and that meant following park district rules. If we didn't, it was not uncommon for bald, paunchy, and normally jovial "Dee" Pierre, who ran the program at Ormsby, to break up a fight or an argument and tell us "to take a hike for a coupla weeks." When we came back, he'd demand an apology because he "just wasn't gonna take any guff from teenage punks."

We tolerated the authority as long as we were winning tournaments, and with our drinking fathers, working mothers, and indifferent teachers, we needed a little discipline. We also trusted and admired a park director like Nick Kostek, who still played sandlot baseball in the Greater Pittsburgh League. Though he was only 5 feet 6¼ inches tall, Nick, who always insisted on that extra quarter of an inch in height, had actually earned a try-out with the Washington Senators in his younger days.

Another park director, Frank Paparella, must have learned from Machiavelli's *The Prince* that if you can't get them to like you, then at least make them fear you. He'd whack us on the back of the head every time he heard one of us use an obscenity. I swore like a drunken steelworker in those days, but I always looked around for Frank before cursing out one of my teammates. He didn't completely cure me, but he was better at teaching me to be "fuckin'" careful with my adjectives than any of my frustrated high school English teachers.

During my years of playground ball, I also discovered an identity that transcended, at least for a few hours each day, my life on the South Side. Like novelist James T. Farrell, a working-class kid from Chicago's South Side, I was going through the same hopeless hope of playing in the big leagues. Like his Studs Lonigan, I went to the ball field to act out the dream of "driving a home run over the center fielder's head and then making one-handed and shoestring catches in the outfield." But, unlike Studs, I avoided, thanks to Ormsby playground and its directors, the life on the streets. I also believed, with an absolute faith, that I could really accomplish things on the ball field that were only brief fantasies for the doomed Studs.

James T. Farrell may have dreamed of playing second base for the Chicago White Sox, but my vision carried me out to center field for the Pittsburgh Pirates. In Philip Roth's *Portnoy's Complaint,* the neurotic Alexander Portnoy, struggling to escape his obsessive feelings of guilt, declares: "Thank God for center field. . . . you can't imagine how truly glorious it is out there, so alone in all that space. . . . Oh, to be a center fielder, a center fielder and nothing more." I felt the same way about center field, though I didn't share Portnoy's guilt. While Portnoy saw center field as an escape and a refuge, I became a center fielder once I started outrunning everyone. But once I ran out to center field and all that open space and chased down fly balls as they floated through the summer sky, I also learned there was nothing as glorious.

By the time I was a teenager, playing center field was everything to me. It was the position I was going to claim when I tried out for the high school baseball team, the space I was going to exploit with acrobatic, death-defying catches that would dazzle bird dogs and scouts eager to sign me to a bonus-baby contract. Every day, I spent hours shagging fly balls at Ormsby playground and Quarry Field. I learned the proper angle to take on balls hit into the outfield gaps, worked on keeping my balance on shoestring catches, and practiced going back on balls hit over my head and catching them over my shoulder. Distrustful of adult coaching, I developed my own style of play—a hustling, daring, aggressive style that would have pleased sore losers like Ty Cobb and John McGraw. I worked hard, played my heart out, risked my neck, and prayed to the baseball gods that someone would take notice once I had the chance to play regularly on my high school baseball team.

When I returned to South High in the fall of my senior year, I did as little schoolwork as possible and cut classes at every opportunity. My schedule was jammed with courses to prepare me for college, but I mostly doodled in class and rarely paid attention. I was so far removed from any thoughts about a future other than playing baseball that I threw away every opportunity for a college scholarship. At one point, our senior English teacher, Miss Wilkinson, gave me a practice test to take home that turned out to be practically the same examination I took on a Saturday morning for a one-year scholarship at Pitt. But I barely glanced at the test before burying it and my future in my high school locker. Several of South High's best and brightest earned scholarships that year, but I didn't and really didn't give a damn. While others prepared to go on to college, I set out to be the starting center fielder on South High's baseball team and the future center fielder for the Pirates.

By the twelfth grade, I'd developed the knack of doing as little as possible into an art form and still made easy "As," but wily Miss Wilkinson had my number. She was so disgusted with my laziness and indifference that she put an automatic "C" and the comment, "lack of effort," on every test and essay I turned in to her. Even when I had one moment of glory and won a five-dollar prize in a Pittsburgh Chamber of Commerce essay contest on "What the Bill of Rights Means to Me," Miss Wilkinson thought it was a fluke, and she was right. My idea of comparing each amendment in the Bill of Rights to a part of the body was original and clever enough, but I hardly made an effort at writing the essay and wouldn't have won a thing if Miss Wilkinson hadn't assigned one of her best students to edit my work. When I won the contest, a frustrated Miss Wilkinson pulled me aside and said, "I don't understand you, Richard. God gave you a good mind to make something of yourself, and you're throwing the gift away."

The big news in the band at the beginning of my senior year was that, after our patchwork appearance and shaky performance at the Pitt Field House last spring, the school administration finally agreed to purchase new uniforms. With our new orange-and-blacks, we now look like the real thing, but we still weren't much of a band. While Mr. Schmidt was busting the buttons of his new director's uniform in pride, we still marched out of formation and played mostly out of tune to an indifferent student body.

After several years of shared embarrassment, my best friends were in the band, but that alto horn had become my high school albatross. I hated that horn so much that I spent most of my time skipping band practice and even ducked out when we had our picture taken in our new uniforms for the yearbook. At fall football games and spring concerts, instead of playing, I'd puff out my cheeks and fake it. I'm sure Mr. Schmidt noticed, but he never said a word. In my senior yearbook, he wrote, "'Chess,' we had a band," because I spent most of my time in band homeroom playing chess. He wrote his comment next to the picture of the band, but that picture didn't include me.

While I went missing in action and spirit for Mr. Schmidt, I also tried to avoid senior events that would expose my insecurities and inadequacies. The winter Sno-Ball dance and the spring Fiesta were the biggest social events, but I'd learn my lesson in junior high about the potential humiliation of going to a dance when you didn't know how to dance. I attended a roller-skating party because at least I knew how to skate, but, when a couples' skate or ladies' choice was announced, I wandered off to the concession stand or the men's room. My old band buddy, Mary Alice, managed to grab me for a couples' skate, but, as great as she looked in her boat-necked sweater and short skirt, I remember how flushed I was and how sweaty my palms were as we held hands and whirled around the floor.

While couples were going steady all around me and slutty stories were circulating in the halls and cafeteria about who was "putting out," I never went beyond developing secret crushes on every cute girl who sat in front or in back of me in class. Since we were seated alphabetically, that meant that my crushes were usually limited to girls with last names that started with "P."

My big mistake was listening to my band buddies when they told me that Mary Jo Polansky who, "the word was," thought I was "kinda cute and funny," would make a perfect date for Senior Prom. When it finally reached the point where Mary Jo's friends told me that she was expecting me to ask her, I picked up the phone, dialed her number, and, in a shaky, high-pitched voice, asked her to the prom. When she said she'd love to go, I knew I'd made her happy, but I also knew Mary Jo was in for a real shock once we got to the dance.

It should have been a perfect senior prom. I doubled with saxophone-playing Chick Gregord and his girlfriend because I had no car, and I couldn't drive even if our family had one. When Chick drove to her house, Mary Jo came to the door looking pretty in pink and, to my own shock, revealing, even with glasses, in her low-cut prom dress. After her older sister, realizing I was so nervous I'd have probably stabbed Mary Jo to death, pinned on the corsage for me, we climbed into the backseat of Chick's car and headed to the Edgewood Country Club.

Our dance band had wonderful music to play at our prom because there were great pop songs in 1956, including a new wave of rock-and-roll hits. Couples slow danced to the vocals of the Four Lads, the Platters, and the Four Aces and fast danced to Elvis Presley and Bill Haley and His Comets. Once we got to the prom, Mary Jo and I stood and watched the other dancers for an awkward stretch of time until the band started playing "Moments to Remember," which had become the theme song for every senior high school class in 1956. Mary Jo said, "We have to dance to this," and dragged me by the hand onto the dance floor. When I put my arm around her and whispered, "I can't dance," she stood so still that she might as well have been a pillar of salt, then took my hand and led me off the dance floor.

Mary Jo was a good sport about my confession, but the rest of the evening went by in a long, embarrassing blur. When we drove back to the street where she lived, I walked her from the car to the front door, but my dream of a goodnight kiss vanished, when Mary Jo, instead of lingering for a moment, fled up the front steps to her house and closed the door behind her without once looking back.

The disaster at my senior prom would have been more tolerable if my high school baseball season that spring had gone according to plan. I had great expectations, but, from my position in center field, I watched our team play so poorly that we looked like we were a high school parody of the last-place Pirates. I also discovered to my frustration and sorrow that a 5-foot 8-inch, 135-pound outfielder (the milkshakes didn't work) was not a high priority for local scouts, who were looking for the next Babe Ruth.

I tried my damndest to get noticed, but there wasn't much I could do in a city league dominated by hard-throwing, erratic pitchers who were more likely to walk you or hit you with a pitch than throw something hittable over the plate. In an eight-game varsity schedule, after struggling because I was trying too hard, I made a few nice catches, but nothing spectacular, banged out a few base hits, but nothing for extra bases, stole some bases, but not the attention of a scout or even a bird dog, and earned my varsity letter, but not a professional contract or even an invitation to a tryout camp. When I finally got my first base hits, Coach Cue patted me on the back and said, "You earned it, Petey, 'cause you worked so goddamned hard for it," but I could have wept because I expected so much more.

When I graduated in June 1956, I'd done enough in class to rank an unlucky thirteenth academically in a class of 220 seniors, but I might as well have finished last. Having just turned seventeen, I had no college scholarship, no baseball contract, no job skills, and absolutely no idea of what to do with myself beyond playing ball. The green cover of South High's 1956 yearbook had the Disney figure of Peter Pan embossed on it. The yearbook editors couldn't have picked a better image to reflect my emotions when I graduated because I didn't want to grow up. South High had never seemed like Never Never Land, but I desperately wanted to believe, as if South Side soot was fairy dust, that Coach Cue would call me and tell me that my double promotions were a big mistake, that I had to go back to South High for another year and play baseball for him. But, that September, when everyone else my age went back to high school, I had to find another way to follow my baseball dream.

With no sandlot team on the South Side, and, without a car, I had to be content with playing pickup games and park district ball for the next year, but the following spring an old South High teammate gave me one more chance to pursue my baseball dream. Portly and cherub-cheeked Sonny wasn't much of a ballplayer, but he was bored and had a car. He told me about a call for tryouts from a Mount Lebanon team in the South Hills League, at that time a magnet for local baseball scouts and bird dogs. The idea of two working-class kids making the roster of a sand-lot baseball team in one of the wealthiest sections of Pittsburgh seemed a long shot, but I desperately needed a team and Sonny was willing to drive the several miles to Mount Lebanon. So for a few weeks in the spring of 1958, I sat shotgun as Sonny drove his beat-up Chevy Styleline out of the working-class South Side, up the 18th Street extension, on our way to ritzy Mount Lebanon.

In the lofty air of Mount Lebanon, a district we mocked as " Mount Cheese and Crackers" because we wanted to believe that you couldn't afford to eat anything else if you owned a home there, I had one of my best baseball springs. After playing high school baseball at South High Stadium, with its brick-hard dirt playing surface, its oblong football field, and its surrounding cinder track, it was a joy to practice in the early evenings at Mount Lebanon's lush baseball field with its perfectly balanced dimensions. Looming far above the South Side, Mount Lebanon became the site of my field of dreams. If Shoeless Joe had emerged out of the surrounding trees and asked if this were heaven, I'd have told him it was just Mount Lebanon, but he'd be very close to the way I felt about that field.

Instead of batting against the backdrop of an ugly, aging school building and the distracting sight and sound of cars whizzing up a ramp leading to the Liberty tubes, I could now pick out the baseball from the greenery lining the field and slash the ball into the outfield gaps. Used to running down fly balls at my own risk because of broad-jump pits, drainage sewers, and head-high fences, I could now lope along in a grass outfield and range far to my left and right without the fear of a broken ankle or decapitation. After practicing at the same time as Fifth Avenue's track team, I could now camp under a fly ball without the danger of being impaled by a javelin or having my skull crushed by a lead shot-put ball.

Knowing this was my last chance to play baseball and attract the interest of a local scout or bird dog, I went all out in practice, played aggressively in intrasquad games, and made the team. For the first time in my career in organized baseball, I was handed a uniform that didn't have South Side or South High stitched on the shirt. After I went with the team to a local sporting goods store to pick out my own bats, I got ready to play center field and hit lead-off for a well-heeled Mount Lebanon team in its first game of the season.

I also had a big problem heading into our opener because Sonny and his beat-up car didn't make the team, and without Sonny I had no ride to the games. But Sonny told me not to get my "ass in an uproar." He "kinda knew" he wasn't going to make the team, but trying out was his idea. He had nothing better to do, so, "what the fuck," if I'd pitch in some gas money, he'd drive me to the games.

My first Mount Lebanon league game was scheduled for 6:30, so a few minutes before five, I gathered up my baseball gear, put it in a shopping bag, and waited for the honk from Sonny's car and my summons to my last hope of a big-league career. I waited for the honk and began to pace, anxiously waited a few minutes more, and finally went downstairs to sit on our front stoop. After an agonizing half hour, I cursed Sonny as a "mother-fuckin' liar" and finally gave up. I went back upstairs, put my bag away with the rest of my athletic stuff, turned on the clock radio, with its hands approaching 6:00, and glumly listened to Tommy Edwards sing "It's All in the Game."

A little after six, less than thirty minutes from game time, I finally heard the honk from Sonny's car. As we snaked our way out of the South Side and up the hill toward Mount Lebanon, I was so upset with Sonny and his excuse about car trouble that I just sat in the front seat, staring hopelessly out at clock after clock in store windows telling me that I was never going make it on time for the 6:30 game. When we finally made it to the ballpark a half hour late, I hustled over to our bench and ignored the puzzled looks of my teammates, who told me we were already down 5–0 in the bottom of the third. I figured I'd be sitting on the bench for the rest of the game, but our unhappy manager told me to go out to center field in the top half of the inning. When I opened my shopping bag to get my glove and put on my spikes, I stared into the black hole of my baseball career. In my rush to get out to Sonny's car, I'd grabbed the wrong shopping bag. Instead of my glove and spikes, I was looking down at my Ormsby basketball shorts and top, my knee-high socks, and a moldy jock strap.

When the bottom half of the inning was over, I discreetly borrowed a glove and headed out to center field, but I didn't get very far. In those homogenized rock-and-roll days, I was sporting a pair of off-white bucks, popularized by Pat Boone. When our manager spotted them, he yelled out at the shortstop to "tell that asshole to get off the field." My reaction, when I got back to the bench, was typical of the way I'd been handling disappointment and defeat since I lost a game of musical chairs fifteen years ago. I unbuttoned my shirt and flung it, Mount Lebanon lettering and all, in the direction of my infuriated manager and told him to shove it up his ass. My parting words in my last day in a baseball uniform, or at least half a uniform, were hardly the stuff of Lou Gehrig's "the luckiest-man-on-the-face-of-the-earth" speech. As I left my field of dreams for the hellish descent back to the South Side, I yelled at my now ex-manager that he'd have to wait for "the fuckin' pants" because I needed them to wear home.

After a long, hot, and frustrating summer of playing pickup games at Quarry Field, I finally had to recognize that I was out of options as a baseball player. So in the spring of 1959, at the washed-up age of twenty, the same age as Clemente in his rookie season with the Pirates, I swallowed my pride, gave up my big-league dreams, and became the player-manager for the South Side Black Sheep, a slow-pitch softball team that my Ormsby playground buddies had organized because they wanted to move up from park district tournaments to the Honus Wagner Softball League.

We were so good, or the teams we played against were so bad, that we had a perfect season in the Honus Wagner League, the bottom tier of the three major softball leagues sponsored by rival Pittsburgh sporting goods stores. In our first season, we wrapped up the championship weeks before the season was over. By raffling off a nonexistent portable radio to a make-believe relative of one of our players, we also came up with the money for leather-sleeved jackets with "SS Black Sheep, 1959, Champs," emblazoned in gold on the jacket's black wool vest. Once we had our championship jackets to wear around the South Side, we figured it would be easy to find a local beer joint willing to sponsor us next year in the more competitive and expensive Allegheny County Softball League. A season after that, we'd be ready to move up to the Greater Pittsburgh League, the highest level of Pittsburgh softball.

Our problem in the summer of 1959 was that we had more bravado than talent. We talked a tough game, but we rarely lived up to the talk. One late Saturday afternoon, we were playing ball at Ormsby when a night watchman threatened one of our teammates who'd tried to retrieve a softball that had gone over the fence and rolled under the gate of a nearby sand-and-gravel company. That night, we decided it was our turn to hassle the night watchman. There was a small opening in the gate, just wide enough for us to squeeze through one at a time. Once inside, as we were creeping around the piles of cement blocks, the watchman suddenly appeared and started screaming at us. We had him outnumbered ten to one, but we panicked and ran for the gate. I was the fastest Black Sheep, so I made it to the opening first. But, in a scene that must have resembled passengers trying to climb into a lifeboat on the sinking *Titanic,* the rest of my teammates piled into each other as the watchman pummeled them on their backs until the last of the Black Sheep finally squeezed himself out of harm's way.

For all our posturing, we really didn't belong in the upper division of Pittsburgh softball. The established teams in the Allegheny County and Greater Pittsburgh softball leagues had more size and experience, even if we refused to see the difference. Most of their players had spent a few years playing semipro baseball, and a few had made their way to the minor leagues. Occasionally, one of the teams would even lure a former big leaguer on to the softball field for a little money on the side. The best hitters in the upper-level softball leagues had nicknames like "Jumbo," "Biggie," "Sluggo," and "Moose." Every middle infielder was a "Slick" and every outfielder a "Rabbit." The best teams had a steady, smooth-fielding second baseman and shortstop, a fast, strong-armed outfield, a "Biggie" towering over first, a "Sluggo" at third, and a "Moose" looming behind home plate. They also had a crafty, veteran pitcher, usually the team's playing-manager, with a name like "King" or "Duke."

We were a team of odd-looking, undersized, overachievers with nicknames like "Buzzy," "Iggy," "Techy," "Chick," and "Carp." We had a player everyone called "Skull," but that was because of his oversized forehead and not because he was dangerous on the field. We had only one jumbo-sized player, and that was "Gus," our overweight catcher, who'd been squatting behind home plate since his Little League days. Gus, unfortunately, wore glasses and didn't like any contact behind the plate. When a runner came charging home, Gus, instead of blocking the plate with his bulk, would step aside like a matador, and swipe his glove as the runner came sliding in.

We thought we played a smart game, but some of us really weren't all that bright. One of the reasons I ran the Black Sheep was that I knew how to spell ethnically challenged names like "Brecosky," "Pingelski," and "Karwoski" in our scorebook. We also had our fair share of South Side oddballs. Every time our first baseman, Iggy, sat down with a hamburger from a local greasy spoon, he declared, "There ain't nothing like food when you're hungry." Iggy also couldn't see very well, so the throws from our shortstop, George, had to hit his outstretched glove or they'd sail right past him. Our left fielder, Jimmy Punk, was brighter, but he had a low threshold for pain and an unfortunate habit of flopping to the ground with an injury whenever he misplayed a fly ball. My mother, who was a regular at our home games, would get mad at me for not running over from center field to see if Jimmy was okay, but Jimmy, without my help or sympathy, always managed to stagger to his feet until his next outfield misadventure.

We were a team that played well because we'd played so much ball together as kids, but we didn't know our physical limitations. As we watched upper-division softball on the nights we didn't have games, we deluded ourselves into thinking we were as good as the more experienced softball teams in Pittsburgh and wanted desperately to prove it on the ball field. Out of all sense and reason, we decided to challenge the best teams in the Allegheny County and Greater Pittsburgh leagues to money games. We had two convenient targets. Landos, sponsored by one of the South Side's drugstores, was the best softball team on the South Side and a long-standing first-division power in the Greater Pittsburgh League. Gene & Rich's, sponsored by a beer joint in Warrington, just up the hill from the South Side, was the first-place team in the Allegheny County League and was loaded with veteran players. We thought both teams had reputations just ripe for the taking if we could get them to play a game against us.

The money game derives from the old city and town rivalries dating back to the nineteenth century, but, on the South Side in the 1950s, it was a way to settle a local rivalry and pick up a few bucks on the side.

It was also a popular event because South Siders liked nothing better than watching a good grudge match. As for Landos and Gene & Rich's, playing a money game against my Black Sheep was an easy decision because they had sponsors to put up their end of the money, which was to be twenty-five dollars for each of the ten starting positions. With no sponsor, we'd have to figure out a way of coming up with the $250 pot for each game, which wasn't easy considering most of my Black Sheep were working jobs for the dollar minimum wage at gas stations, greasy spoons, and five-and-tens, or collecting unemployment checks. For most of us twenty-five dollars was more than a half-week's pay. If we lost both games, it would cost us over a week's wages.

But the biggest challenge, once each of us came up with his share of the pot, was keeping up our confidence going into the games. We had our share of big mouths and bullies, but, as the games approached, the few levelheaded Black Sheep thought we were making a big mistake. Buzzy, our roving shortstop, who, unlike most of us, had a decent job and a steady girlfriend, pulled me aside and said, "We got a snowball's chance in a steel mill of beatin' those guys." As far as Buzzy was concerned, Iggy and some of the other guys were "too goddam dumb to know better," but I "shoulda had better sense" than to book money games with the likes of Landos and Gene & Rich's.

I thought Buzzy was dead wrong about our chances, but he was right, at least about Landos. When the game started, it was as if Einstein had tampered with the physics of playing softball. The balls we batted for base hits in the Honus Wagner League were cut off before they bounced through the infield holes or were caught before they sailed into the outfield gaps because Landos' fielders got such a great jump on the ball. Ground balls we'd fielded routinely in the Honus Wagner League shot through the infield before we could move a step, and fly balls we'd easily reached in the outfield now soared far beyond our grasp.

At one point, after I managed to run down a towering drive in right-center field, I watched helplessly as the next drive sailed over the left-center field fence and disappeared into the night. As the score mounted from 6–0 at the end of the first inning to an unlucky 13–0, the only mystery left in the game was whether we could score a run against Landos. We did get three gift runs in the last inning on a couple of errors, but lost the game 13–3, along with our money and our pride.

After the game was over, I changed out of my spikes and into the penny loafers that had replaced last year's off-white bucks, then had to listen to threats from the team's loud mouths unless I figured out a way to get us out of the money game with Gene & Rich's next week. But, for all the threats, we played the game because the ridicule we'd face on the South Side for welshing on a bet was far worse than the pain and embarrassment of another lopsided loss.

So we scrounged up another $250 and lost our money again, though this time we didn't embarrass ourselves and even gained back a measure of respect. Gene & Rich's players were bigger and older but not that much better, and they certainly weren't in the same league as Landos. We scored some early runs, made some good plays in the field, and led in the early innings before finally losing a close, hard-fought game to a more experienced team. After losing the Gene & Rich's game, we were disappointed and frustrated, but we didn't feel humiliated as we had after the Landos game. It cost us twenty-five dollars a player to learn the hard lesson that Landos in the Greater Pittsburgh League played in a far different softball universe than we did, but, for another twenty-five dollars, we found out, in our close loss to first-place Gene & Rich's, that we could compete in the Allegheny County League.

We were broke and, for the next few weeks, discovered, by deprivation, the simple truth behind Iggy's logic that there truly is nothing like food when you're hungry. But the Allegheny County League was now beckoning us into the decade of the sixties, and we had until next season to recover our fallen spirits and finances.

In the spring of 1960, just as the Pirates were beginning their miracle World Championship season, we found a South Side beer joint to sponsor us and became a fully uniformed entry in the Allegheny County League. But, after a great start as Club Café, we struggled against better, more experienced teams and ended up in the bottom half of our division. At the end of the season, and only a year after our losses in the money games, we did manage to win something called the B-Level Playoff, but it was nothing more than a series of games to decide who was the best of the worst in the Allegheny County League.

Our Club Café sponsor, a squat, bulldog-faced bar owner named Moe, tried to recoup his investment in a losing team by forcing us to peddle tickets for an end-of-the-season raffle. When we refused to go along,

Moe, whose favorite expression was "boys, yunz gotta shit or get off the pot," dropped his support of the team for next year and demanded his uniforms back. With no sponsor, no uniforms, and no reputation, we became the Black Sheep again and muddled on for another season in the Allegheny County until Yanks Sporting Goods threatened us with expulsion. Without uniforms, we'd become an eyesore on the field and, without a sponsor, a financial liability off the field. At the end of the season, I finally gave up on my lost Black Sheep.

As my ball-playing days on the South Side were dwindling down, I didn't know that, game by game, I had been gathering memories of moments that would serve me well when life became more complicated than winning or losing a ball game. Years later, when my ball-playing days had been reduced to Saturday afternoon softball outings, I discovered that I could ease my way out of thinking about mid-life crises and anxieties, especially late at night, by recalling clean base hits and running catches from my South Side days. As I grow older, those remembered base hits and catches have become less and less of a dreamy escape and more and more the tender fabric of my emotional life. If Marcel Proust was right and we discover our true nature in the memories of moments of elevated emotion, then a good measure of my emotional life flows from the remembrance of perfectly placed hits and perfectly timed catches from what now seems like a never-ending flow of ball games from my youth.

Chapter 7

In 1960, Pittsburgh, after its postwar renaissance, experienced another transformation, but it had nothing to do with the social, political, and cultural dynamics that would change the Levittown fifties into the Woodstock sixties. Rather than Martin Luther King and John F. Kennedy, the names that made a difference in Pittsburgh at the beginning of the decade were those of baseball players. In the summer of 1960, Pittsburgh's long-suffering baseball fans put on their "Beat 'em Bucs" buttons, headed out to a jammed Forbes Field, listened to the Benny Benack band play "The Bucs Are Going All the Way," and rooted for Dick Groat, Vernon Law, Roberto Clemente and the first-place Pittsburgh Pirates, as the team played its way to a World Series Championship, the first for the city in thirty-five years.

Several days into the 1960 baseball season, a few of my old Black Sheep teammates and I went out to Forbes Field for an Easter Sunday doubleheader and watched the beginning of the Pirates' miracle season. After paying a buck for seats in the left-field bleachers, we watched Roberto Clemente hit a two-run, first-inning home run as the Pirates went on to an easy 5–0 first-game victory over the Cincinnati Reds. Between games, we waited until the ushers were distracted and slipped through the gate separating the bleachers from the general admission and reserved section. We stayed in general admission for most of the second game, but in the late innings, with the Pirates losing and fans beginning to leave the ballpark, we worked our way down to the reserve seats along the first-base line. By the bottom of the ninth, we were sitting comfortably in deserted box seats just behind the Pirates dugout.

The Pirates made it easy for us to find empty seats in the better sections by playing so poorly after winning the first game. There were about 16,000 fans in attendance at the beginning of the doubleheader, but, by the bottom of the ninth of the second game, only a handful of die-hards were left in the stands. From our box seats, we watched the Pirates go into the bottom of the ninth trailing 5–0, but, with one out in the inning, they started a rally. After three straight singles cut the lead to 5–1, Hal Smith, a backup catcher destined to become a World Series hero, hit a towering pitch-hit home run over the left-center field wall to cut the Reds' lead to 5–4. One out later, Dick Groat, who would become the National League's Most Valuable Player in 1960, bounced a single into center field. Left-fielder Bob Skinner, down to his last strike, lofted a fly ball that hit the top of the thirty-foot screen in right field and bounced into the stands for a two-out, two-run homer and a 6–5 Easter miracle victory. As Skinner circled the bases, my buddies and I rushed onto the field and joined a small mob of fans waiting to pound him on the back when he crossed home plate.

In Les Biederman's coverage of the game in Monday's *Pittsburgh Press*, Bob Skinner said, "All I did was hit the ball, and when it went into the seats, I knew the game was over. . . . I put my head down and ran and when I looked up all I saw was kids. They seemed to come from all directions and converged at home plate."

To my astonishment, the photograph beneath the story of the mob scene at home plate, shows me standing barely two feet from Skinner as he crosses home plate and shakes hands with Roberto Clemente. As for Clemente, despite the excitement of the game and the drama of the early season, nothing much had changed in the way he was depicted in Pittsburgh papers. When asked to describe Skinner's home run, "a chattering Roberto Clemente" supposedly shouted, " 'I bet you . . . that 'Doggie's' ball she bent iron bar over the right field fence. That's how hard she hit, son-o'-mo-gun.'"

That miracle finish on Easter Sunday, so unlikely for Pirate teams accustomed to losing and so unexpected by Pittsburgh's long-suffering fans, became a trademark of the 1960 season and, with its dramatic home runs, a precursor to the seventh game of the World Series. The Pirates not only started to win games, they surged into first place and

Game-winning home run celebration, Easter Sunday, 1960 (courtesy of the *Pittsburgh Post-Gazette*)

stayed there all season. They were a scrappy, come-from-behind ball club, perfect for an underdog steel-mill town. With so little to cheer about for years, Pittsburghers, after years of estrangement, embraced their baseball team and flowed out to Forbes Field to watch their born-again Bucs.

I remember going out to Forbes Field that summer and, after years of watching the Pirates in a mostly deserted ballpark, shaking my head in disbelief at all the fair-weather fans with their gaudy banners and funny hats. The Pirates' pennant-winning season was thrilling, but, after years of having the run of Forbes Field, I wasn't all that happy with the crowds that filled the ballpark and forced me farther and farther back into the stands. By the end of the season, it became very difficult to buy a ticket for a game and impossible, even if you had a ticket, to sneak into the better sections of the ballpark.

Frontrunners or die-hards, Pirates fans were witness to a miracle season. For old-timers, like my father, who were kids when the Pirates played in their last World Series in 1927, it was a joy and a relief that the Pirates had won another pennant in their lifetime. For those of us who grew up thinking we would never see the Pirates play in a World Series, it was like living a dream. And to top it off, after winning the pennant, we were to play the Yankees in the World Series, the same damn Yankees that had swept and embarrassed the Pirates back in 1927.

Pirates fans can tell you exactly where they were on October 13, 1960, when Bill Mazeroski drove Yankee pitcher Ralph Terry's second pitch over the 406 mark in left-center field and gave the Pirates a 10–9 win and the World Series championship. For Pittsburghers, the memory of the game remains so perfect that, over the years, hundreds of thousands will tell you they were at Forbes Field on that memorable day, even though the ballpark's seating capacity was only 35,000.

I was twenty-one years old and still living in Pittsburgh in the fall of 1960. I saw Mazeroski's home run, but I was miles away from Forbes Field when he hit it. Like thousands and thousands of Pirates fans, I couldn't get a ticket for the seventh game of the World Series, so I went to work that morning at Gimbels department store in Downtown Pittsburgh. An unhappily employed stock boy, I watched the seventh game that afternoon in the furniture section on Gimbels' tenth floor with my new friend Bud, an equally unhappy stock boy, along with a crowd of buyers, salesmen, and secretaries.

Mazeroski circles the bases after 1960 World Series–winning home run (courtesy of the Pittsburgh Pirates)

After watching Mazeroski hit his dramatic home run and cheering his black and-white romp around the bases, Bud and I rode the escalator down to the first floor and hurried out of Gimbels through the Saks Fifth Avenue employees' entrance. We emerged onto Sixth Avenue just in time to see a snowstorm of toilet paper streamers, IBM cards, typing paper, and even an occasional phone book cascade out of the windows of office buildings.

We spent the next several hours wandering along Sixth and Smithfield as a flood of Pittsburgh workers, who normally wouldn't give each other the time of day, snake-danced in streets so deep in confetti that streetcars had to plow their way from stop to stop, and streamers caught fire on the electric lines. Workers were soon joined by thousands of other Pittsburghers flowing across the bridges into the Downtown area for the celebration. After a few hours, the streets were so jammed with celebrants that the police closed the tunnels leading into Downtown Pittsburgh in a desperate and futile attempt to keep people away.

Bud and I spent most of the late afternoon and evening drifting along with the wild celebration and watching the bizarre sights. We also made occasional stops at the Brass Rail, where the blue-collar workers from Gimbels usually hung out after work, and the Cork and Bottle, where the shirt-and-tie Gimbels executive class put in their after-hours. We toasted the Pirates with drafts of Iron City at the Brass Rail and hugged and kissed willing sales girls, then sponged free shots of Seagram's at the Cork and Bottle and hugged and kissed stuck-up female buyers and assistant buyers, too drunk to realize we were only stock boys until it was too late.

Well after midnight, Bud finally staggered off to his home in Esplen, and I wove my way back to the South Side. The next morning, I barely dragged myself and my large hangover back into Downtown, past somber buildings and exhausted street cleaners, and headed to Gimbels for the 10:00 A.M. opening bell. When I got to my assigned floor, I was greeted with an icy stare from a grumpy, raven-haired assistant buyer from Interior Decorating, who, Pirates or no Pirates, obviously wasn't happy when she woke up and realized she'd kissed a lowly stock boy the night before.

I could hardly blame any female with self-respect and ambition for being unhappy about kissing the likes of me in the fall of 1960. Because of the Pirates, there was magic in the air, but I was no Gimbels frog prince. My stock-boy job was the accumulation of four unhappy, humiliating years of failed jobs, beginning right after high school with pumping gas for a dollar an hour at Hoder's Gulf station on the South Side.

I'd been around gas stations all my life because that's how my father made his living, when he was sober enough to make a living. But horsing around gas pumps and grease racks as a kid hadn't prepared me for working with my father at Hoder's. Just out of high school and barely seventeen in the fall of 1956, I'd never driven a car, never changed a tire or fixed a flat, couldn't grease a car or change its oil, knew nothing about working on failing brakes or leaking transmissions, and wasn't interested in learning. But once I'd loafed my way through the summer after graduation, my mother said I had to do something with my life besides playing ball and watching the Pirates—so she told my father, "you better talk to Jim Hoder about gettin' your do-nothin' son there a job."

Lean and hungry looking, Jim Hoder was wary of hiring Frankie Peterson's kid, but he needed all the help he could get at the gas pumps. In 1956, gas was cheap and America was in the middle of a love affair with V-8–powered gas-guzzlers. Even working-class South Siders were buying, usually on time payments, those oversized monstrosities with their toothy grills and gaudy tail fins.

On my first morning at the job, after pulling on an ill-fitting, oil-smelling Gulf coverall, Hoder told me that my main responsibility was the gas island. "When you hear that bell ringin'," he said, "come runnin' like hell." When there were no cars at the pumps, I was to keep "the crapper" clean, the oil and paper towel racks filled, and, occasionally, whitewash the curbs. I also had to wash and Simonize cars in the back garage, including the black Cadillac Seville owned by Father Walter, the St. Casimir's parish priest who doubled next door at St. Joseph Hospital.

While doing all this, I had to follow Hoder's rules. There was to be no portable radio in the station, not even for the World Series. Because of Hoder, I missed Don Larsen's perfect no-hitter that fall against the Dodgers. Hoder also didn't believe in taking time out for lunch, at least not for me. Around noon, he'd let me run across the street to Bianchini's for an Italian sausage sandwich, but I had to eat it in between waiting on customers, while Hoder sat in the back garage, eating the lunch he'd brought from home. Above all, Hoder made it clear that there was to be no rudeness at the pumps, no matter how obnoxious the customer. For Hoder, the customer, who was paying twenty-five cents a gallon for regular gas and usually getting a free set of something or other in the bargain, was "king" and his car was his "castle on wheels."

I was so miserable at Hoder's that every time a South Side king and his castle rolled into the station, I mumbled a "fuckin' asshole" under my breath and dragged myself out to the gas island. Hoder's instructions were to greet the customer with a smiling, friendly "fill 'er up with No-Nox or Crest?" but unless Hoder was watching, I glowered in silence at the driver and hoped he'd tell me he wanted only a buck or two of regular Gulf because I hated filling up the gas tank. In the 1950s, "fillin' her up" should have qualified a gas station attendant for hazardous pay because gas-station pump handles in those days had no automatic shutoff valve. If you didn't pay attention, and I seldom did, the tank would fill up and shoot gas back up the line. The gas would overflow and spill down the back bumper or tail end of the car, not to mention soaking your shoes and socks and staining the driveway.

Hoder's instructions also included cleaning the windshield and politely offering to check the oil; but I made a point of ignoring the dirty windshield and forgetting about checking the oil. If the poor driver was foolish enough to ask me to clean his windshield, he had to sit there and watch me use a soapy Gulf spray that transformed South Side soot into an oily film. If he had the nerve to remind me to check his oil after I smeared the windshield, I fumbled with the hood release, if I could find it, puzzled over the location of the dipstick, then tried to figure out how to read the oil gauge. Usually I told the driver "the oil looks okay," no matter what the gauge read, took the money to a suspicious Hoder, then watched the car, with its dripping gas stain, wheel its way back out of the gas station—looking for all the South Side as if it had peed itself.

The only pleasant memory I have from my year in Hoder's gas station started out as a winter nightmare when Hoder asked me to stay on with my father for the evening shift because of an approaching snowstorm that was threatening to turn into a blizzard. If we stayed, Hoder could leave for his home in the suburbs while the roads weren't that bad, and my father and I could walk the few blocks to our home, once Eddie, our midnight relief, made it to the station

The storm, for all the warnings and Hoder's fear, was nothing like the Thanksgiving blizzard of 1950 that paralyzed Pittsburgh and forced the National Guard to use tanks as snow plows, but, by early evening, it was bad enough to frighten South Side drivers into a frenzy of panic buying at the gas pumps. Over the next few hours, as the snow intensified and formed a carpet on the driveway and helmets on the island pumps, it seemed that every driver on the South Side was heading into Hoder's for a few extra gallons of gas just in case the city shut down the next day. As I worked the pumps, I kept shoving dollar bills and coins into my soaked coveralls until the deep pockets bulged with money.

That night, at least for a few hours, I was so caught up in the whirlwind of snow and the delirium at the pumps I forgot how much I hated my job at Hoder's. At times, it seemed like I was caught up in a holiday parade of every make and model of car imaginable, as Ford Fairlanes and Chevy Bel Airs, Olds 88s and Buick Roadmasters, Hudson Hornets, Nash Ramblers, and even an odd Studebaker and Willys Aero, slid up to the pumps. The line of cars seemed endless, but I never felt tired or cold, or even aware of the time passing, until Eddie turned up around midnight to relieve us. By then the snowstorm had wound itself down to flurries, the traffic and customers had just about disappeared, and the South Side looked deserted and ghostly. I didn't realize, until I emptied out my pockets and changed out of my wet coveralls in the warmth of the station house, that I was exhausted.

After my father read the pumps, we left the gas station, and began walking home through an amazing winter transformation. The deep snow had buried all traces of the grime from the J & L steel mill, and the crisp night air seemed momentarily free of the sour odor from the Duquesne Brewery. The sidewalks, alleys, and streets appeared to brighten and glow as we passed through the arcs of light at the street corners.

When we reached Wharton Street, my father stopped in front of Kalki's because he wanted to thaw out with "a few boilermakers" from the tips he'd made putting on tire chains. He said, if I wanted to come in with him, "maybe I can get Kalki to spike your Coke." I thought about it, remembered my mother's warnings about "becomin' just like your old man," and just shook my head. My father shrugged, turned his back on me, and disappeared into the smoke and heat inside the beer joint.

When I got to Merriman Way, it was as if I'd wandered into a pure, flawless world, remote from gas stations and beer joints. The deep snow had transformed the scrap yard and the sand and gravel company into silver silhouettes and slopes. It had covered the alley's ugly, uneven bed of red bricks and tar patches and obscured the run-down houses and empty lots. The next morning I'd have to trudge back to work through snow coated with soot and streaked with grime and follow the arc of my life back to another miserable day at Hoder's. But for now I was surrounded by an uncommon beauty and stillness for the South Side. When I got to my grandparents' house, I paused long enough to make a few snowballs, hurled them into the night air, and watched them disappear. Before I went upstairs, I took one last look up the alley for my father, but all I saw were my own footprints.

I stayed on at Hoder's through a cold, dreary winter of misery and discontent, but in the spring of 1957, I lost my job over some missing money. Every so often, when Hoder went over his books, he came up short. My father told me that Eddie was probably writing down false figures from the pumps when he came in for the midnight shift, then pocketing some of the gas money for drink. He wasn't going to say anything to Hoder "cause the cheap bastard's gettin' what he deserves."

When my father didn't show up for work one morning and disappeared for a few days on a spring bender, Hoder finally decided he knew where the money was going and fired my father. The next day he also decided he could do without "the son of a thief." So he fired me, got rid of my surliness and incompetence, and saved a dollar an hour in the bargain.

I was glad to escape Hoder's, but, while my father found another gas station job on the South Side and Eddie kept stealing Hoder blind, I spent the next year failing at everything. I barely lasted a few months working with my cousin at a paper box factory, where flying sheets of cardboard cut razorlike gashes into my fingers and hands. After that ordeal, I was so unhappy and desperate that I try to enlist in the Navy, but, when the doctors asked me to stand at attention, they discovered my scarred left elbow. After they realized that I couldn't straighten out my arm, they huddled up, told me, "Son, it looks like you're not physically fit for military service" and declared me 4-F.

Unqualified for a decent job and unfit for the service, I wandered around Downtown Pittsburgh, looking halfheartedly for busboy jobs at cafeterias and five-and-tens. When that failed, I signed up for unem-ployment checks and took an aptitude test that said I'd make a good city park director. I'd return home by 4:00 and try to escape into the world of the slow dance, the stroll, and rate-a-record on Dick Clark's *American Bandstand,* but that only reminded me of my high school disasters on the dance floor.

No matter how badly things went for our family, my mother, who kept things going despite the failings of her husband and son, said we'd always have enough food in our bellies, as long as she worked, and a roof over our heads, as long as my grandparents were alive and will-ing to put up with us and my father's drinking. But, my grandmother Petrauskas, who always seemed to be praying without result for our family, clutched her rosary beads at St. Casimir's early Mass and keeled over with a fatal heart attack.

A few months later, I found my grandfather lying in an icy puddle near the piles of junk he kept and guarded so religiously in the back-yard. Within a few weeks, he was dead of complications from pneu-monia and a broken hip. After my grandfather's funeral, my father's older brothers and sisters told my indifferent father and disbelieving mother that they were putting the house up for sale. We had a month to move out of the upstairs rooms.

My mother had every reason to be bitter about her family. Her brooding husband had used the death of his parents to go on another drinking binge. Her moody son couldn't or wouldn't help out by finding steady work, and my sister was beginning to show adolescent signs of resentment at being ignored by her father and big brother. And to top it off, my father's own family had evicted us. But after a good cry and with the help of her two sisters, my mother packed up everything, which wasn't very much, and rented the first floor of a run-down house a few blocks away on Nineteenth and Carey Way.

Moving away from Merriman Way meant leaving behind the world of my childhood, but, as disruptive as the move seemed at the time, the substance of our lives didn't really change all that much. My mother kept working, though, with rent to pay, she left her job waiting tables at Rodger's for a better-paying job stuffing kielbasa in the refrigerated air of Arsenal Meats out on Polish Hill. My father had to find a new job and a new beer joint to replace Kalki's, but on the gas-station and beer-joint polluted South Side that was no problem. And I kept drifting between ball fields and the unemployment line until one of my father's relatives intervened in our lives again.

When we left Merriman Way, my mother blamed my father's oldest brother, Joky, for instigating the sale of the house. She was also mad at my father's kid brother Tony because he "didn't have the goddam backbone" to stand up to Joky and didn't care what happened to us. But my Uncle Tony, who worked at one of Gimbels' South Side warehouses, apparently did feel bad and told my mother he'd try to help out. To my dismay, his way of helping out was to find a job for me as a stock boy at Gimbels' Downtown department store. Tony, who, with his ski-nose and beer belly, resembled a working-class Bob Hope, was a nice guy and my favorite uncle, but all the good memories of playing catch down in the alley and talking about the Pirates while we washed his car were in serious jeopardy when I found out about my new job at Gimbels.

Gimbels Brothers was located in a massive fifteen-floor building at Sixth and Smithfield in the heart of Downtown Pittsburgh and catty-corner from the newly constructed Mellon Square. It had two lower levels for its bargain basement sales and eleven floors for items ranging from first-floor accessories to eleventh-floor bedroom furniture and toys. The twelfth floor was a honeycomb of bins loaded with irregular stock eventually headed for sale days, and the unlucky thirteenth floor had a company cafeteria, where workers ate their brown-bag lunches or, if they could afford it, bought badly prepared and tasteless meals.

For the first few months at Gimbels, I was a grumpy and unhappy drone in a department store beehive. Whatever department had a sale, that's where I was sent to unload hampers from the freight elevator and stock the floor displays. As a stock boy, I was making $1.15 an hour, barely more than the minimum wage. I usually worked less than forty hours a week and had to take at least one day off each month so I wouldn't qualified for the union by working thirty straight days. The only good thing about the job was that the hours didn't interfere with my ball playing. I usually worked from the 10:00 A.M. opening bell until 5:00 P.M. and had just enough time to catch a bus or streetcar for the South Side and make it to a 6:30 game.

The stock-boy job wasn't hard work, except when we were moving furniture, and at the end of 1959, it actually became fun for a few months when I was assigned to Toys on the eleventh floor. Christmas season in Downtown Pittsburgh, with its gala window displays at Gimbels, Kaufmann's, Rosenbaum's, and Horne's, officially opened in the 1950s on the day after Thanksgiving. From the moment Gimbels closed on the Wednesday before Thanksgiving to the opening 10:00 A.M. bell on Friday, the store was a maze of activity, but especially on the eleventh floor.

The toy section normally occupied a small space on the eleventh floor near the express elevators, but for the Christmas season all the bedroom furniture and mattresses were moved down to the tenth floor, so Toys could be expanded to cover the entire top floor of the store. To get everything ready, we worked through the late-night hours on Wednesday, came back on Thanksgiving Day, and stayed through Friday morning. We wheeled dressers and carried mattresses down to the tenth floor, unloaded hamper after hamper of toys brought up on the freight elevators to the eleventh floor, set up display after display of everything from Barbie dolls, tea sets, and doll houses to Lincoln logs, Legos, and erector sets, then topped it off with a throne fit for Santa Claus.

That holiday season, I actually went to work early just so I could play with the toys before the opening-bell rush of customers ascended on the express elevators and attacked the floor displays. During store hours, we unloaded endless hampers of toys dumped out of the freight elevators, loaded up cart after cart, then wheeled them through aisles of frenzied shoppers, and filled the shelves in advance of the next assault. But, before the morning opening bell, we had the toys all to ourselves. I spent year after year of my childhood dreading Christmas because my mother had to struggle to find the money for gifts, and my father made it worse by seeing the holiday season as an excuse for drinking himself out of a job. But for the 1959 Christmas season, I had every toy imaginable at my fingertips.

At the age of twenty I was a born-again kid, but this time with a wonderland of toys waiting for me on a Christmas morning that kept repeating itself. I had Lionel trains to run, medieval castles and frontier forts to defend, and Schwinn bikes to ride up and down the aisles. My stock-boy buddies and I also had a dazzling display of sports action games to play. We lined up miniature football players in a flying-wedge formation, turned on the electric current, and watched the figures spin off in every direction except straight ahead. We pulled back levers and lofted an orange-colored Ping-Pong ball toward small, plastic-corded basketball hoops, though if you pulled back too hard the ball sailed over the backboard and bounced across the linoleum-covered floor in the dangerous direction of the escalator. We also played fierce hockey games by sliding levers back and forth and sending tin players up and down a metal surface until one of them knocked the oversized wooden puck into the slot inside a small, plastic goalie net.

I told the Gimbels Santa Claus to bring me the sports action games for Christmas, but I had my own plans for another sports item. It was pretty routine, if you were a low-paid stock boy, to steal things from Gimbels. There was a store detective stationed at the Saks Fifth Avenue employees' entrance, and store policy clearly stated that all employees should come and go, under watchful eyes, through that entrance. But stock-boy policy was, if it fit under your clothes, you could steal it.

All you had to do was take the back stairs a few minutes before closing time and slip through the revolving doors at the Sixth and Smithfield main entrance with the paying customers. On one occasion, three of my ball-playing buddies walked into Gimbels in their worst pair of shoes, went up to the twelfth floor, where I showed them bin after bin of slightly irregular off-white bucks headed for a sale on the lower levels. When they left the store through the Sixth and Smithfield entrance, they looked for all Downtown like a backup group (though slightly irregular) for Pat Boone.

That Christmas I had my eye on a newly issued set of plastic baseball figures, eight inches tall, but perfectly detailed and posed. There was a determined Hank Aaron in his batting stance, a graceful Willie Mays making his famous basket catch, a crafty Warren Spahn in full delivery, and even Pirate Dick Groat in his closed stance—and they were just small enough to conceal inside my coat. A decade ago, my mother had thrown a fit when she found the glass figurines I'd shoplifted from a Downtown five-and-ten, but this time she bought my lie when I told her the buyer in Toys had given the baseball figures to me "as a Christmas bonus." She proudly set them on the bedroom mantel, where they stayed for years until she finally gave them away to a neighbor's kid, and before I discovered that those $1.98 figures had become rare collectibles, worth hundreds of dollars apiece.

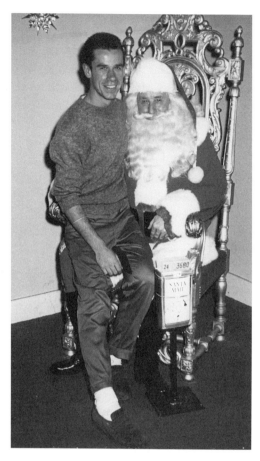

Gimbels stock boy, 1958

Once the holiday season was over, I helped to dismantle the toy department, and then was sent down to Draperies on the ninth floor. After all the Christmas fun and excitement in Toys, Draperies, with its hampers of blinds, shades, and curtains, and its tables of drapery bolsters, decorative pillows, and slipcovers, seemed like a department store limbo. But boredom was only half the problem in Draperies. The other half was working every day with the head stock boy, Joe Nardi.

Even before my banishment to Draperies, I knew all about Nardi because he was so disliked by the other stock boys. He was older, had a noticeable Italian accent, a sinister hooked nose, dark curly hair, and wore a white shirt and tie to work as if to distinguish himself from the rest of the stock boys. At lunch, if anyone dared sit at his table in the cafeteria, he'd act as if you weren't there. He'd just keep reading his *New York Times,* while the rest of us, unworthy of Nardi's company, read the funnies and the sports section in the morning *Post-Gazette,* talked about the Pirates or the Steelers, and ridiculed Nardi from a distant table.

For several weeks Nardi lived up to his reputation and all but ignored me, but by the spring of 1960, he'd become less surly and even began using me as a sounding board. In the morning, Nardi liked to eat bagels from the first-floor bakery shop when he was on his break. Once I joined him, and with no *New York Times* to use as a shield, Nardi started in on everything from his general disgust with America to his personal contempt for everyone connected with Gimbels.

In between savage bites from his bagel, Nardi demanded to know what I knew about politics, which was very little, and the arts, which was even less. With America about to elect a new president in 1960 after eight mind-numbing years of "Mamie's bangs," he asked if I were going to vote now that I was turning twenty-one. He also thought it was time I started reading about something more than sports and gave me odd books, with names on the covers like Lenin, Plekhanov, and Marx and Engels, and all printed by International Publishers.

After deciding that I actually had a brain in my head, though I hadn't made much use of it, Nardi thought it was "fuckin' ridiculous" that I hadn't gone to college. During the summer, while the Pirates streaked toward the National League pennant and Presidential politics heated up, Nardi, who knew nothing about baseball but lusted over the idea of Jackie Kennedy replacing Mamie Eisenhower as the First Lady, started his own campaign to get me out of Gimbels and off to college. By late fall, in the afterglow of the Pirates' World Series victory over the Yankees and Kennedy's close election over Nixon, Nardi started to get through to me. After four years of lousy jobs, even I began to realize it was time to do something unless I wanted to be a stock boy for the rest of my life.

When I talked to my mother about college, she flatly said, "You're outta your goddam mind." She wanted me to get into the union at Gimbels instead of coming up with "a lot of foolishness" about going off to college. But Joe Nardi, who was reading Sartre and Camus at the time, insisted it was time for me to make my "existential leap" out of Gimbels, and Sam Calderone, another of my stock-boy buddies, made the leap seem practical and possible. Business-minded, mild-mannered

Sam, who was working at Gimbels for a year to earn the money for college, kept feeding me information about applications and loans and explaining how easy and inexpensive it was to attend a Pennsylvania state teachers' college. Nardi wasn't thrilled about the loyalty oath I'd have to sign for a National Defense loan, but he was willing to set aside his fears of big-brother government and join forces with Sam if it got me back to school.

I listened to Joe Nardi's radical rhetoric about living the authentic life and Sam Calderone's practical encouragement about going back to school, but I also had a new friend to include in the advice I was getting at Gimbels. I'd first encountered Bud when we worked together in Toys, but I really didn't get to know him that well until I went to Draperies after Christmas and Bud was assigned one floor down in Appliances.

At first I disliked Bud as much as I had dreaded working with Joe Nardi. With his black wave and long sideburns, Bud, who lifted weights and took wheat-germ pills, looked like a Charles Atlas version of Elvis Presley. He was grabby with the salesgirls in the back stockroom and a bully with the other stock boys. But the more I got to know Bud as we helped each other out on sale days, the more I realized that, like Nardi, he was mostly bluff. After a while he even became part of our morning bagel break and offered some relief from Nardi's Marxist politics and existential posturing with stories of his sexual escapades.

Working and hanging out together, Bud and I looked like a Gimbels Mutt and Jeff, but we gradually became friends, despite Bud's blustering and bullying ways and his inexplicable love for hillbilly music at a time when rock and roll was all the rage. Bud loved "guitar-pickin'" Chet Atkins, thought "yodlin'" Hank Williams was the god of country singers, and believed Elvis Presley was great because he was a hillbilly in his heart, if not in the way he moved his hips. When we cruised around Pittsburgh on a Saturday night in Bud's beat-up DeSoto—his "bedroom on wheels"—he'd blast the Grand Ole Opry on WEEP and sing and yodel along with Slim Whitman and Eddy Arnold. When even the sleaziest-looking girls refused to get into the car with a sex-crazed yodeler bellowing out "your cheatin' heart," Bud and I would just drive around and talk, though mostly Bud did the talking.

I'd listen to Bud's stories about visiting the "cat houses" along the lower Hill District and the whores "who'd go round the world" but wouldn't kiss you on the lips. I'd hear all about the latest jailbait in Bud's neighborhood or about some "hot-to-trot" married Gimbels salesgirl who was always rubbing against him in the back stockroom. Bud even had a favorite story, a gang bang in the backseat of his DeSoto, that seemed to increase in numbers at each telling until Bud and his pals, in my imagination, became sex-crazed clowns climbing in and out of a circus jalopy.

In response I nodded knowingly at Bud, but his tales of sex in whorehouses, abandoned lots, and the backseats of cars were far beyond my own experiences. It took a couple of years out of high school, but I finally fell out of my movie fantasies and into my first real crush after a magical summer night's kiss from a tennis-playing tomboy from Ormsby playground. We went for long walks around the South Side and had a great time just talking, but Judy, with her bobbed light-brown hair, bedroom eyes, and great-looking legs, was going to back to high school in the fall and, while I seemed to have nothing much going in my life, she had cheer-leading, dating, and eventually marrying a basketball player in her own future.

A little later, I actually went steady for a few months with another girl from Ormsby and spent winter evenings fumbling under her coat at a Gimbels' loading dock on the South Side, just around the corner from Ormsby. Bev sometimes let me go where I had never gone before, but her idea of a really good time was going downtown to the county morgue to gaze at the unidentified bodies fished out of Pittsburgh's rivers and lying under glass for public display and identification. I never told Bud that my first "steady" seemed more interested in cadavers than with me, for fear that our next stop, at the risk of the clap, would be the stretch of whorehouses along the base of Pittsburgh's Golden Triangle.

Bud, for all his wild tales about sex, also had a troubling story to tell, and its telling had as much to do with my decision to go back to school as anything else in my life. Bud's problems began in junior high when he shot up in weight and height all out of proportion to his age. He compensated for his confusion and clumsiness by becoming a public school terror. He claimed he was in the principal's office so much that they finally made it his "fuckin' homeroom." When he turned seventeen, Bud decided to drop out because he felt he'd "suffocate" if he couldn't get out on his own. But, once he quit high school, he had trouble keeping a job because he began to feel things closing in on him again. And here he was, working at Gimbels where the small space in the stockrooms and the freight elevators sometimes made him feel as if he were being "fuckin' buried alive."

When Bud got around to my own glum situation, he told me I needed to listen to that "crazy dago" Nardi and go to college. As we drove past J & L's, he said the mills were there for "dopes" like him, but not for someone with a "a goddam brain in his head." He didn't mean any disrespect for my family, but I was the one who told him how good my father was "at figures and shit" and how he was wasting his life working in gas stations, hanging out in beer joints, and brooding the night away at the kitchen table.

Bud wanted to know "what the fuck was keepin' me on the South Side." Sooner or later, I'd knock up some girl from the neighborhood, if anyone would have my "sorry ass," and end up married and raising a brood of kids. And some day, if I didn't leave, "we'd be sittin' on bar stools, drinkin' Iron City, and pissin' our lives away." We'd bullshit each other about "what great fuckin' ball players we was," lie about "all the pieces of ass we picked up," and wonder "how we got so fuckin' old."

Bud and Joe Nardi kept bugging me about going back to school until I finally decided to follow Sam Calderone's advice and apply to one of the area's state colleges. I still had to pick a school, so I closely followed the state college basketball scores in the paper. I was a point guard for the Ormsby Park District tournament team and for a Gimbels team in Pittsburgh's Industrial Basketball League that had two former Pitt players on it, so I thought I was a good enough to play college ball, but maybe for a bad team. When Edinboro State College finished with the worst college basketball record among western Pennsylvania's state colleges, I applied to the school and, to my amazement, was accepted for the fall semester.

That spring, I took a bus from Pittsburgh to Edinboro for a campus visit. That bus ride of one hundred miles was the longest trip of my life to that point and the first time I'd ever traveled outside the Pittsburgh area. The trip to Edinboro was an emotional blur, but I can remember taking part in an informal scrimmage between high school recruits and varsity players and doing well enough to believe I could play college ball if given the chance. And I remember walking past a girl's dormitory, as wolf whistles and cries of "fresh meat" descended from the upper floors, and thinking this was going to beat the hell out of trying to pick up girls with yodeling Bud and his bed on wheels.

In the summer of 1961, as I nervously waited to go off to college, Joe Nardi, despite John F. Kennedy's close victory and Jackie's glamorous ascent to First Lady, decided to return to Italy and seek his fortune as the next Michelangelo. Months earlier, when I pressed him about his own inauthentic existence as a stock boy, he'd brought in a *New York Times* article on artists supporting themselves with mindless jobs, while they saved the best part of themselves for their creative work. He was now ready for his own leap of faith.

Sam Calderone, as practical as ever, worked his way through the summer and read books on business during his lunch hour to get ready to attend Indiana State College. And Bud, with nowhere to leap except into more trouble, thought about giving the Army "a fuckin' hard time," though, with his claustrophobia, he was convinced he'd be assigned to a tank unit. I filled out my college forms, saved my money, and waited anxiously for the fall.

As the date for going to college approached, my mother, who'd spent most of her life struggling to survive the present, sat down at the kitchen table and talked to me about my future. My mother wasn't going to tell me what to do with my life, but she wanted me to know what she thought now that I was definitely going back to school. She didn't understand this college business and hoped it wasn't "a lot of damn foolishness," but I had my "father's brain" and maybe it was time I used it.

My mother was worried about the money for college, but then she was always worried about money, so that was nothing new. Besides, she knew that Ben would help me out if I got into trouble. She wanted me to make something of myself, even if it meant going away. But she hated to see me leave and just hoped, with this college business, that I wouldn't forget her or the South Side. It was where she grew up with her brothers and sisters, where she met my father and raised Nancy and me, and where I'd bury her some day.

My mother worried that I'd forget her, but that was her own foolishness. Whatever hard work and perseverance, stubbornness and pride I was going to need to succeed in the world beyond the South Side, I inherited from my mother. She was the one who had the tough-mindedness to keep the family together when everything seemed ready to fall apart. And she was the one who cared about me, even when I gave her reasons not to care, and took pride in the few good things I'd accomplished as I was growing up.

But I was also my father's son and inherited his way of looking at the world. College was my chance to escape my father's bitterness and regret, but the only real difference between us was that I had the good fortune of meeting a few people who thought I was better than a stock boy. I was ready to leave the South Side, but I was taking with me my father's tendency to withdraw emotionally from those around him, even those in his own family.

Chapter

In September of 1961, a little more than five years after graduating from high school, I left Pittsburgh to attend Edinboro State College. The school was located in a small town in northwestern Pennsylvania, about a hundred miles north of Pittsburgh and twenty miles south of Lake Erie.

Besides its college, the town of Edinboro, founded in the late eighteenth century by a native of Edinburgh, Scotland, consisted of two L-shaped blocks highlighted by a post office and a combination convenient store/gas station located in the center of town. It also had a bookstore, a barbershop, and a bakery. There was one movie theater, aptly called the Best, because it was the only show in town. Edinboro had two diners, the Crossroads, famous for its pecan pie, and Liz's, where college students, desperate for comfort food, could order a hot meat loaf sandwich with greasy french fries smothered in thick gravy. On weekends, after dancing at the student union or seeing a movie at the Best, college couples could sip Cokes, smoke cigarettes, and hang out at the Driftwood, while older students drank pitchers of beer at Troy's or Teray's, though the latter was more of a hangout for townies.

Located in the valley of the Conneauttee, an Indian name meaning "snowplace," Edinboro was usually buried from late fall until early spring with lake-effect snow cascading down from Lake Erie. But, with its small lake, Edinboro became a modest resort town in the summer, especially for middle-class families from Pittsburgh, who often decided to send their children to college at Edinboro after vacationing there. When students from Pittsburgh and environs arrived in September

Edinboro winter, 1965

for the fall semester, females were housed in dormitories or lived with families near the campus, while males, with the exception of freshmen living in the newly constructed Centennial Hall, stayed in drafty lakeside cottages, which were strictly off-limits to females. On a Saturday night, most of the cottages were completely dark and appeared deserted until just before curfew when a chorus of car engines started up, hundreds of headlights came on, and sweaty and rumpled couples joined a lakeside traffic jam of cars frantically heading back to the dorms.

I went to Edinboro to play basketball, but, when I enrolled for classes, I also had to pick a major course of study. In 1961, Edinboro had just changed its name and status from Edinboro State Teachers College to Edinboro State College, but for the most part it was still part of a system of Pennsylvania public schools, ranging from Slippery Rock to Cheney, for training elementary and high school teachers. Unlike Slippery Rock, Edinboro, best known for its art program, had no physical education major, so most of its athletes, looking for the academic path of least resistance, gravitated to social studies. When I showed up at Crawford Gym to register for fall semester and saw all the jocks in the line for social studies majors, I decided there had to be something better than sitting in class with linebackers and wrestlers. The most attractive and interesting-looking young women were standing in the line for English majors, so I figured if I got into trouble there were always those *Classics Illustrated* comic books that got me through high school. Without the remotest idea that I was making one of the most important decisions of my life, I became an English major.

A skinny 5 feet 8½ inch walk-on, I didn't last long on Edinboro's basketball team, but the disappointment didn't overshadow the beginning of a remarkable change in my life from high school to college. After being younger than my high school classmates because of my two double promotions, I was now, at the age of twenty-two, four years older than most of the freshmen at Edinboro and about the same age as its seniors. I was also healthier than at any time in my life because, after years of playing ball and eating on the run, I was living in the freshman dorm and eating three balanced meals at the campus cafeteria in Haven Hall, including a family-style supper on weekdays that required a suit coat and tie for male students and a dress, nylons, and heels for females. I was also burning my lungs out, running the back roads of Edinboro all winter, in a determined effort to get in shape to run track after failing to make the basketball team.

Being older than other students paid off immediately and unexpectedly, when my freshman English and Speech professor, who looked like she was just out of college herself, kept staring at me after calling out my name on the first day of classes. When my English class was over, she called me up to her desk, told me I reminded her of someone, and asked if we had met somewhere before. When I told her I didn't think so, she just smiled and said it was her "silly mistake" and she'd see me in Speech. I think the main reason I got an A in both English and Speech that fall semester was that my attentive professor must have been fond of that "someone" from her past. One afternoon, when I was walking from campus to the post office, she pulled over in her car and offered me a lift, which was rather odd because the post office wasn't much more than a block away. When I got into the car, I thanked her for picking me up. When she asked if I were "an easy pickup," I realized, to my embarrassment and confusion, that she might have had playing post office on her mind more than driving me to the post office.

A walk to the post office, when my English professor wasn't picking me up, was actually part of my daily routine. There were no athletic scholarships at Edinboro, so those involved with sports were given jobs. My good fortune was that I landed a job as one of a handful of campus mailmen. Every morning and afternoon at Centennial Hall, we sorted through the mail and, after distributing letters in the boxes for the freshmen male students, headed out to deliver and pick up the mail at the female dorms. Being a mailman was easily the most popular and enviable job on campus. As we sorted through the mail, I was gaining valuable insider information on the love life of female students. If a girl was receiving letters with the stamp upside down, it meant she had a steady boyfriend back home. If the stamp was sidewise, she was, at best, dating someone. If all she was getting were regular letters from her family and friends, she was fair game at the student union.

There was also an added bonus when it came time to deliver the mail. My first and favorite stop was East Hall, which wasn't much more than a World War II barrack masquerading as a dorm, but it housed some great-looking young women. Every morning, I opened the door to East Hall and walked into an overheated waiting room filled with scantily clad females anxiously looking for their letters. It was like walking into the pages of *Playboy*. All I could see, as I dropped off the mail, or all I can remember seeing, were short robes, flimsy nighties, and lots of skin. Once, when I was eating supper at Haven Hall with a few female English majors from East Hall, they asked if I knew one of their friends. I stopped eating, looked under the table, and said, "I recognize the legs."

I dated several wild-eyed, neurotic English and art majors from East Hall and had some modest success with lines from John Keats's letters to Fanny Brawne on the sorrow of unfulfilled passion. But it was a sweet elementary education major with Kim Novak's looks and Doris Day's disposition that proved my undoing in my freshman year. Shortly after being elected vice president of our class, the result of younger students mistakenly believing that being older somehow made me wiser, I met Anita Homich at the Student Union, just after she'd come back from Saturday evening Mass at Our Lady of the Lake. When religious-minded Anita said she lived in East Hall, I resisted looking down at her legs and telling her she looked familiar. Instead, remembering my English professor's line, I asked her if we had met somewhere before. When a Chubby Checker record started up, I invited her to dance, but she told me that good Polish Catholic girls "didn't do the Twist." She did, however, slow dance with me, so we began our relationship, not to Chubby Checker's "The Peppermint Twist," but to Henry Mancini's "Moon River."

We dated a few times, seemed to get along, but I was born to lose Anita. I learned that, while she was going out with me, she was also dating our freshman class president, known as "the Greek." He was no Adonis, but he had enough charm and good looks to be elected president and apparently win Anita's deeply devout but fickle heart. Rumors started to circulate around campus that she was trying to decide between becoming first or second lady of our freshman class. The rumors caught me by surprise because I didn't feel that dating meant I was in a relationship, but, no matter what I thought, the rest of the campus saw it as a juicy love triangle and put pressure on Anita to make a choice. While she made the right political decision by dumping me, I was so angry about the whole business that I didn't speak to her for a year. A few years later, I'd finally get my revenge by asking Anita to marry me.

I recovered from my adventure with my English professor and my misadventure with Anita and went on to make the dean's list and the track team in my freshman year. In the spring, I also decided to pledge a fraternity because social life at Edinboro was practically nonexistent unless you belonged to a fraternity or sorority. There were four major fraternities at Edinboro, and each one had its own character. The Delta Sigs had a reputation for drinking and partying, while the Sig Taus were known for their sobriety and seriousness. There wasn't much choice when it came to the Kappa Delts and the Phi Sigs. Both attracted the athletes on campus, though the Kappa Delts, by just a hair or two, seemed the more Neanderthal of the two.

The sororities were ranked, at least by the fraternities, by their looks and reputation. The Alpha Gams, the sister sorority of the Delta Sigs, were regarded as party girls, while the Alpha Delt, the sister sorority of the Sig Taus, were the kind of girls you could take home to mother. The other two sororities, the Zeta Taus and the Rho Chis, were devoted to good works, but their reputation, at least among frat guys, was for attracting girls who looked like your mother.

When pledge week came around that spring, I was expected to go Sig Tau, and, if Anita, who went Alpha Delt, hadn't dumped me, I probably would have done it because I had my own reputation for seriousness and sobriety at Edinboro. While I rarely took a book home in high school, I studied into the late hours at Edinboro. Remembering my father sitting at our kitchen table and smoking and drinking his life away, I wouldn't touch a cigarette and rarely took a drink. After being cut from the basketball squad, I ran daily, even in the bitter cold, placed in the 440 and the mile relay, and earned my letter in track.

The Sig Taus seemed like an obvious choice for an older but wiser freshman, but I decided that it was time to start having a little fun and pledged the Delta Sigs. There was no Animal House at Edinboro because there were no frat houses, but, if there had been, the Delta Sigs would have been living it. Their reputation as a party fraternity was not only well earned, it was a matter of pride, at least for the Delta Sigs. Delta Sig keg parties at rented lodges were legendary for turning into marathon bouts of drinking and debauchery. The fraternity was also notorious for showing up intoxicated at a Greek Sing and belting out, "There Ain't Nothin' Like a Dame." Dating a Delta Sig was risky business for any female, but being pinned to a Delta Sig was regarded, at least in the eyes of other sororities, as a clear sign of lost virginity and respect. There weren't many athletes among the Delta Sigs, but they did invite their Delta Sig chapter from Gannon in Erie for an annual touch football game, appropriately called the Grain Alcohol Bowl.

I had my first revelation of what it meant to be a Delta Sig when, as a pledge, I went on a road trip with one of my big brothers. We may not have had a frat house, but the Delta Sigs at Penn State had one with a wonderfully wicked reputation. The house was called the "Pink Elephant" because the basement, where the serious drinking and partying took place each weekend, had a pink elephant painted high up on the wall. Circling the wall of the basement were other pink elephants, each one tilted more than the one before it. The last pink elephant was painted upside down. Legend had it that when a Delta Sig and his date, after drinking and dancing their way around the basement, came to the last pink elephant, instead of being upside down, it would still appear right side up.

When we arrived on campus, our Penn State brothers fixed us up for the Saturday night keg party. As nervous as I was, I couldn't have asked for a better date. Dressed in a tight black sweater and clearly out for a good time, my date drank and danced her way around the pink elephants as if she'd met them before, then whispered in my ear that she thought I was cute and we should go somewhere to be alone. In my drunken state, all that I could think of, besides sex, was my big brother's parked car. So we kissed, grinded, and groped our way up to the main entrance, which, in my beer-soaked vision, was now the portal to sexual paradise.

When we opened the door, we staggered out into a driving rainstorm and quickly staggered back, as if someone had throw buckets of water on us. For the rest of the evening, I drank myself into oblivion, but, even in my drunken haze, I thought it curious, for someone who still didn't know how to drive, that I had begun my freshman year trying to find a polite way of getting out of my English professor's car and was ending it by nearly drowning my date in a ill-timed attempt to get into the backseat of my big brother's car. I started out the evening feeling like a fraternity Adam, drinking and dancing with an apple-polishing Eve, but I ended the night with a cold shower more fitting for Job.

When my freshman year was over, I went back to Pittsburgh and my old routine of playing softball and working at Gimbels, though things weren't the same on the ball field or in the stockroom. My Black Sheep team, after barely hanging on without a sponsor, money, or much talent, was now a bad softball memory, so I become a softball mercenary, playing for different teams around the city as long as their sponsors offered free beer and sandwiches after the ballgames.

At Gimbels, I returned to a deserted stock room. Joe Nardi was in Rome, Sam Calderone was probably off earning his first million, and Bud had lived up to his threat by enlisting in the Army. I did receive one postcard from Joe telling me to "study hard and get laid," but, even though I wrote back, I never heard from him again. Bud and I didn't write, but I knew from his mother that things weren't going well and that it was only a matter of time before the Army bounced him out of the service on some sort of discharge. There was a new secretary at Gimbels who made life in the back stock room entertaining during breaks. She also went on an extended lunchtime field trip with me to the Fort Pitt Hotel, which was only a block or two from Gimbels. It was the same hotel where I'd attended a luncheon award banquet in my senior year after winning a prize in an essay contest and where I'd agonized over an unfamiliar-looking salad and the extra forks beside my plate. Lunchtime at the Fort Pitt this time around was far less confusing and a lot more appetizing.

At home, my father still drifted from gas station to gas station in between benders, while my mother kept the family afloat with her steady job stuffing kielbasa at Arsenal Meats out on Polish Hill. She was still seeing her longtime boyfriend, Ben, but was now more open about the relationship.

No matter what, we always seemed to muddle along, at least until my first summer home from Edinboro. For the past few years, my sister's way of compensating for the lack of an emotional relationship with her indifferent father and self-absorbed older brother had been to turn to the growing attention she was getting from boys in high school. A willowy, dish-water blonde with her mother's pale, flawless complexion, Nancy, now eighteen years old, had dropped out of high school a year earlier and was now running around with a rough crowd. When I came home from Edinboro, my mother warned me that Nancy was "gonna get herself in trouble" because she was seeing someone much older, but I was too caught up with my own life to really worry or care about my sister.

A few weeks later, I'd just finished playing a softball game at Ormsby playground when one of my buddies asked if that was my mother coming across the street. When I saw her, I knew something terrible must have happen because she was crying. My mother rarely gave in to her emotions and never in public.

When I ran up to her, she showed me a crumpled sheet of paper and, in between sobs, told me what had happened. "He stole my baby," she cried. "That no-good, sonavabitch stole my baby." She sat down on the concrete steps leading up to the field and held out Nancy's note in appeal.

"She says, don't worry Mom. She wants me to be happy for her. . . . How could she be so goddam stupid, runnin' off with a sonavabitch worse'n your father?" She looked at me and pleaded, "So now what'll I do? How'm I gonna get her back?"

There was nothing I needed to tell my mother. In a few weeks Nancy turned up with her new husband and, several months after I returned to Edinboro for my sophomore year, she had the first of two children. The "sonavabitch" she ran off with was a small, wiry Irishman from up the hill in Mount Oliver. His ill-tempered father and brothers loved their drink, and my sister's new husband was no exception to the Irish stereotype of the drunken hooligan. Still a teenager, Nancy had married an abusive version of our brooding, alcoholic father, but, with grandchildren to protect, our mother forgave her, tolerated her husband, and formed an even stronger emotional alliance with her daughter. I was far less forgiving of my sister, but for our mother's sake, I accepted an uneasy truce until Nancy's next emotional catastrophe.

When I returned to Edinboro for my sophomore year, I was determined to have my own good time. Instead of staying in a freshman dorm, I was living in a lakeside cottage with two of my fraternity buddies. On Saturday, I'd drink all afternoon at keg parties, then wander up on campus to reconnoiter the new freshman at the women's dorms. My hunting license was a "church key," a beer-can opener that I proudly wore around my neck when I was on the prowl. When one of the new freshmen at Reeder Hall started flirting with me and calling me "Peter the Wolf," I knew I'd be hunting for her that evening in the Student Union.

Picking up girls at the student union and getting them down to Lakeside wasn't very difficult if you had a car. The local policeman did patrol the lake, but he was so dim and ineffectual that students called him "Snowball." My problem was that I didn't have a car, so that meant walking to lakeside in snowy frigid weather and looking over my shoulder for headlights. When a car did appear, I'd push my disbelieving date into a snow bank, then pull her out once the car drove by. By the time we made it to the cottage, she looked like an abominable snow woman, but after an apology and a few beers to thaw us out she melted back into a real live girl.

While my love life was on the upswing, I discovered that my drinking and fooling around weren't hindering my academics. My grades actually got even better in my second year at Edinboro. I also discovered that I was enjoying the courses in my English major, especially Dr. Marsh's American Literature class. I'd never read much more than comic books and pornography, both blamed for teenage delinquency when I was growing up, but I discovered that I now liked reading the serious literature that I had resisted in high school. I'd spent my breaks at Gimbels that summer reading novels, poetry, and plays from Dr. Marsh's advanced reading list, and, though I couldn't make much sense out of Faulkner's *The Sound and the Fury,* I fell in love with Ernest Hemingway's hard-boiled dialogue and F. Scott Fitzgerald's extravagant prose. I also discovered that James T. Farrell's Chicago South Side wasn't all that different from Pittsburgh's South Side, but if I had to die young I preferred to go out like playboy Gatsby rather than the sickly Studs.

Dr. Marsh was everything you could ask for in an English professor. He affected Sherlock Holmes in his dress and mannerisms and had the biting wit of Oscar Wilde. He lectured with a great baritone voice that sounded like a combination of Lowell Thomas and Cecil B. DeMille. He also scared the living hell out of his students, who sometimes felt they were listening to the voice of an angry academic God. We were on the semester system at Edinboro, so, after Christmas, we still had to go back to turn in our term papers and face final exams. On the last day of class before the holiday break, Dr. Marsh informed us that, while we were heading home, he and his wife would be sitting by the fire, roasting marshmallows, and listening to the radio for the latest accident reports. He urged us to speed home on the icy highways because every fatality meant one less term paper and final exam he would have to read.

I had my own unfortunate experience with Dr. Marsh at the beginning of the semester when a student knocked on our classroom door and handed an irritated Dr. Marsh a letter from the Dean of Students for Richard Peterson. Dr. Marsh pointed an accusing finger at me, but, when I was handed the letter and opened it, I found nothing inside. My big mistake was raising my hand to tell Dr. Marsh that the envelope was empty. He smiled, looked at me as if I were the perfect straight man, and boomed out, "Maybe it's an indication of what's in your head."

I had my revenge on Dr. Marsh several weeks later when we were discussing *The Seven Year Itch,* one of the plays in a Modern American Drama collection that included *Death of a Salesman* and *A Streetcar Named Desire.* Dr. Marsh loved to sprinkle his lectures with questions that he was sure no one in his class of cultural illiterates was capable of answering. In *The Seven Year Itch,* a comedy about a May-September flirtation, the infatuated middle-age hero plays "The September Song" on the piano for an attractive young woman renting the apartment just upstairs, a role Marilyn Monroe and her billowing skirt made famous in the movie version. When Dr. Marsh asked if anyone knew where "The September Song" had originally been performed, I raised my hand in class for only the second time and told him it was from the musical, *Knickerbocker Holiday.* A stunned Dr. Marsh tried to recover by asking me the name of the actor who performed the song, but I had him dead in my sights and informed him and the disbelieving class that it was Walter Huston.

What I didn't tell Dr. Marsh was that I knew the answer because, in my unemployment days in Pittsburgh, I used to listen in the afternoon to Art Pallan, a KDKA disc jockey who occasionally played a golden oldie and gave a bit of historical background for the song. I was just happy that Dr. Marsh now thought that maybe I had something in my head after all. At the end of the semester, after escaping the icy highways between Pittsburgh and Edinboro, I turned in a term paper on "The Mature War Play" that Dr. Marsh published in *Debut,* the college literary magazine.

While my academic career was taking flight, my athletic career was falling victim to lakeside living and fraternity bashes. After eating a balanced diet of dorm food my freshman year, I was now living on the five-pound rings of bologna from Arsenal Meats that I lugged back from Pittsburgh after each visit home. During the week, I'd slice the bologna into sandwiches for lunch, then fry it up and eat it with a can of baked beans for supper. If I ran out of bologna, I'd buy or shoplift a can of Spam from the local grocery. I had plenty of gas in those days, but not the kind to propel me around the track. I still made the track team, but this time I was so out of shape that I failed to earn enough points at meets to letter again.

I was also distracted from any serious thoughts of training by a new girlfriend. Marie was an attractive, short-haired freshman art major who clearly came to Edinboro to have a good time. When we started making out for the first time at my lakeside cottage, Marie looked around and said, "So, this is how it's done." I weakly protested, but kept on going because she was right. When things got a little hotter, she whispered in my ear that she didn't think she'd make it through Edinboro without getting pregnant, a casual comment that had the same chilling and sobering effect on me as that rainstorm at Penn State a year ago.

It was a relationship founded upon hormones and alcohol. When we were sober, we had difficulty putting up with each other, but when we drank, our relationship, though a bit hazy, seemed like the greatest thing since bologna and baked beans. Our problem was that we had to get through a week of not getting along before a weekend of heavy drinking and fooling around. When things really heated up between us, Marie told me I could have anything I wanted in exchange for my fraternity pin, but I kept hesitating because I wasn't sure that I wanted to be the reason she didn't make it through Edinboro.

That summer my unpinned girlfriend went home to a small town on the shore of Lake Erie, and I headed back to Pittsburgh to work at Gimbels and play softball. We were still going together and wrote each other a few letters, but we couldn't get along even by mail. I did make one visit, but, after going to one of Marie's hangouts and watching her make eye contact with several of her old high school boyfriends, I knew that she was having a good time that summer, pin or no pin. To get to her place, I had to take a bus from Pittsburgh to Edinboro and then hitchhike the rest of the way on the interstate. I did catch a ride, but it was with a state trooper who explained to me that hitchhiking was illegal on the interstate. But, when I told him I was doing it for love, he drove me the rest of the way. It must have been a proud moment in the life of my girlfriend's already-worried parents when their daughter's college boyfriend arrived for a visit in a state trooper's car.

Though twenty-four years old in the summer of 1963, I still couldn't drive a car, but all that changed by the time I headed back to Edinboro for my junior year. My mother told me that one of her Arsenal coworkers wanted to get rid of an old car that was cluttering up his driveway, so Ben drove us out to Polish Hill to have a look. The car turned out to be a huge-looking 1953 Oldsmobile 88 with a tan body, dark brown roof, and a dark blue replacement fender on the driver's side. The car was a giveaway at $35, but, after Ben paid for the car, the old owner had to drive it to the South Side where it sat until I got my learner's permit. Though my father probably knew who bought the car for me, he was willing take a look at its engine and told me the car looked "a hellava lot better on the inside than it does on the outside." That September, after a few weeks of narrow escapes driving around the South Side and with only a learner's permit in my pocket, I drove the hundred miles to Edinboro for my junior year.

With its dark-blue fender, my Oldsmobile 88, dubbed "the death mobile" by those who were foolish or crazy enough to get into the car with me, became the most identifiable car at Edinboro. The car, however, didn't salvage my already shaky relationship with Marie, which ended the first night back after we parked out on one of Edinboro's back roads. When I tried to make out, a pouty Marie whispered in my ear, "I'm not in the mood," and pointed at my fraternity pin. It was the year of the first James Bond movie, but, with no ejection button in my aging Oldsmobile, the best I could do was drive back on campus and deposit my now ex-girlfriend at her dorm.

A few weeks later, after a touch football game, one of my new lakeside roommates told me that my "old freshman flame," Anita Homich, had dumped her boyfriend, a "swell guy" and Navy veteran. Ray, who had an odd, slangy way of talking about females, said Anita had a good-looking "gourd," a nice "rack," and great "wheels," but she had no business hurting his drinking buddy. I'm sure Ray told me all this out of respect for his friend, but I saw it as a long-delayed chance to patch things up with Anita after our freshman-year fiasco. After finding out that she was living off-campus with the family of one of Edinboro's faculty members, I drove to the house, knocked on the door, and asked for Anita, who actually seemed glad to see me when she came out of the house.

After one of those awkward "long time no see" and "whatcha been up to" conversations, I pointed to the death mobile and asked if she'd like to go for a ride. Instead of gasping in horror and telling me that a good Catholic girl didn't ride in a bedroom on wheels, she climbed into the car and let me drive her around campus, which took all of about fifteen minutes. When we drove back, she seemed pleased that I hadn't run anybody down or crashed into a tree. Before she went back into the house, she turned and said she hoped to see me again, "cute, dark-blue fender" and all.

It wasn't easy, but Anita and I did start seeing each other again. We survived a shaky first date, Anita's bout of mononucleosis, a presidential assassination, and the disapproval of everyone from my friends, who thought I'd get more action dating a nun, to Anita's parents, who regretted that they hadn't sent their daughter to a nunnery after finding out that her new boyfriend wasn't Catholic and was from the wrong side of Pittsburgh.

Our first date was a road trip in the death mobile with two other couples to a Dave Brubeck concert. When Anita climbed into the car, she discovered two jugs of whiskey sours on the floor that the other couples had brought along for fortification during the sixty-mile ride to Grove City College. I thought she'd be mortified, but she smiled at me and asked why there weren't three.

A little more than an hour and a few drinks later, we rolled into a crowded Grove City where the only parking space was a perfect fit for a Volkswagen. We were running late for the concert, so I solved the problem by parking my oversized Oldsmobile at a forty-five-degree angle. After Anita laughed and said we shouldn't have any trouble finding our car, we wobbled off to the concert. Because of the popularity of "Take Five," Dave Brubeck was "cool" on college campuses in the early 1960s, but in an overheated, overcrowded college gym, he didn't seem so cool that evening. As we sat high up near the rafters, Anita also confessed, after a few numbers, that she didn't "understand" jazz, but she was happy that I'd asked her to the concert. We spent the rest of the evening ignoring Dave Brubeck's riffs and getting to know each other. By the time we wove our back to Edinboro, we'd decided to keep seeing each other, though without all that jazz.

The only problem with seeing each other was that Anita developed mononucleosis after a few weeks and was sent home for bed rest. But her bout of "kissing disease" actually helped our relationship. While she was recuperating at her home in Coraopolis, located about twenty miles west of Pittsburgh, I spent my evenings in the library at Edinboro busily doing her class assignments.

In the 1960s, Edinboro's curriculum for future teachers was divided into three parts. We took a third of our courses in our major and another third in basic studies courses, including composition, speech, and introductions to various arts and sciences. The final third of the curriculum was made up of education or what we called "Howdy Doody" courses. They ranged from educational philosophy, where we read John Dewey on practical reasoning, to educational psychology, where we studied B. F. Skinner's behavioral experiments with rats. In a course called General Instructional Techniques, we learned the proper use of colored chalk and how to write on the blackboard while facing the class. We were also taught how to run a projector and splice film in Audio Visual Aids. But more than anything else, we had to read articles in education journals and write up summaries on 4X6 note cards. We received points for the reports, so the more reports we turned in, the better the grade. It was the "educationese" triumph of busy work over critical and imaginative thinking.

When Anita returned to campus, she was well fortified with penicillin and 4X6 cards, so we had no trouble getting back to our own busy work of getting to know each other. On weeknights, we'd study and talk together for a while, then drive out to one of Edinboro's deserted back roads. At our first Delta Sig party, Anita, knowing that, during my F. Scott Fitzgerald, gin-drinking phase, I once showed up with one date and left with another, shackled us together with a pair of toy

With Anita, Inter-fraternity dance, 1963

handcuffs. Anita was just the opposite of Fitzgerald's wild, unstable Zelda, but, under her innocent aura, there was an intelligent and passionate heart and a sly sense of humor. It was going to be easy to fall in love with Anita, but I worried and wondered if someone with her good sense could ever trust and love the likes of me.

Despite the warnings from friends and family and our own fears that we were a mismatch, Anita and I began having the time of our lives. We were also discovering, to my relief, that the more we saw of each other, the more we looked forward to seeing each other. We didn't mind alienating our friends because we were becoming each other's best friend. In a few months we went from two people who seemed to have nothing in common to a couple that cared only about the world we were creating for ourselves.

One of the things that happened to me in my years at Edinboro was that I was paying less and less attention to the news when I returned to campus each fall. I seldom watched television, listened to music on the radio, and rarely bought a newspaper. With the exception of the Cuban missile crisis in my freshman year, world affairs barely made a ripple my life. I even lost track of my Pirates and Steelers, though they weren't that exciting in the early 1960s anyway.

All that changed in my junior year just as Anita and I were getting ready for Thanksgiving break and our first major confrontation with her parents. I was driving around campus on my Friday afternoon mail pickup, when I heard a news bulletin from Dallas reporting that shots had been fired during a presidential motorcade. There was also an unconfirmed report that President Kennedy had been hit by the gunfire. By the time I finished my pickup, the news breaking from Dallas confirmed that the president had been shot, but there was no report on his condition. After dropping off the mail, I frantically ran across the street to Troy's where a crowd of students had already gathered in front of the television set. I sat down on a bar stool, ordered a Coke, which I never touched, and watched and waited until a devastated Walter Cronkite told the nation what no one wanted to hear—that President Kennedy was dead.

That weekend was a blur of shock and disbelief. Anita and I mourned for the Kennedy family, for his wife and his two young children, and wondered how something like this could happen to a president who seemed so loved and admired by the American people. We worried about the country's future, but couldn't begin to imagine that President Kennedy's death, which seemed so personal and profound that weekend, was just the beginning, that what lay ahead for the country for the rest of the decade would be far more devastating than the loss of Camelot.

Anita and I had planned to talk with her parents during Thanksgiving break about the seriousness of our relationship, but we decided, because of the assassination, not to see each other until we returned to Edinboro. So we stayed apart and, with the rest of the nation, watched President Kennedy's funeral. I can remember all those striking images that have now become a part of America's collective consciousness—the young grieving widow placing her wedding ring inside her husband's coffin, the small fragile son saluting his father's passing body—but more than anything else, I can still hear the steady, mournful beat of the drums as the funeral caisson slowly rolled its way down Pennsylvania Avenue to Arlington Cemetery.

When Anita and I returned to Edinboro, we retreated even more deeply into our own private world. We bought wedding rings at a five-and-ten store in Erie and wore them as if we were a married couple. We named our children, all seven of them, and decided to find teaching positions near Edinboro instead of returning to Pittsburgh and family after graduation.

The only serpent threatening our happiness lurked a hundred miles away in Coraopolis. Anita's middle-class parents had raised their daughter as a devout Catholic within a tight Polish family circle. She was also closely watched and protected as a child because she had a serious hearing loss. It didn't help matters for me that her parents were close friends with their next-door neighbors, whose son had been dating Anita off and on since they were teenagers. Anita's parents had let their daughter go off to college, but they were firmly convinced that she'd return to marry the good Catholic boy next door and live happily ever after within their protective family circle.

I was their worst nightmare. They wanted a secure middle-class life in the suburbs for their daughter. What they got, when I walked into their lives, was a beady-eyed character who liked to dress in black, and my three-toned wreck of a car didn't help matters. While Anita tried everything she could think of to convince them that they were wrong about me, they made Anita's life at home a living hell. At the end of our junior year, things looked so bleak for us that we threw our wedding rings into Edinboro Lake and headed back to Pittsburgh, where Anita's parents would have an entire summer to break us up.

That summer I drove the twenty miles from the South Side to Coraopolis almost every evening and was greeted by Anita and an otherwise empty house. When we returned, Anita's mother, no matter how late the hour, would be sleeping on the couch so we couldn't have any time alone in the living room. All summer Anita listened to her parents argue that I wasn't good enough for her and that they hadn't raised their daughter and sent her off to college to marry beneath her. There were even darker hints that the only real attraction between us was sex. I spent many nights that summer in Pittsburgh consoling a distraught Anita, and, despite her family's unrelenting pressure, we managed to hold on to each other until the fall semester. On our last night in Pittsburgh, instead of playing in a critical softball playoff game, I took Anita to the Cork & Bottle in Downtown Pittsburgh to celebrate our survival and plan our future.

When we returned to Edinboro, Anita accepted my fraternity pin and we began to talk about our marriage. We also had to endure another separation because we had student teaching assignments that were twenty-five miles apart. During the fall semester, I was able to stay in a lakeside cottage in Edinboro, while teaching, or trying to teach, seventh graders in Albion, a small town located five miles down the road from Edinboro. I'd spent the past three years reading a steady diet of great writers in my English classes, but at Albion I had to teach adolescent classics, like Felix Salten's *Bambi*. On my first day of teaching, out of sheer panic and desperation, I had my students hopping and prancing around the room as if they were bunnies and fawns.

While I spent my weekdays shuttling back and forth between Albion and Edinboro, Anita was living with her aunt in Erie, while she taught kindergarten in one of Erie's public schools. She had a wonderful time and was a great success, but her most memorable moment came when one of her homesick kindergarten kids ran out of the school building. Anita took off her heels and in her nylons chased down the student before he could get to a street corner. When she told me about her mad dash, I offered her my letter in track and suggested that she start jogging with me on the back roads of Edinboro just in case it happened again.

Anita and I spent our weekdays apart, but on weekends I'd drive up to Erie and, after a stop at Mazza's, a pizza parlor that had a sing-a-long every Friday evening, we'd drive back to Edinboro for the rest of the weekend. By the end of the semester, I'd earned enough money from working weeknights in the campus library to buy an engagement ring. Just before Christmas, we drove back to Edinboro and parked in front of the faculty member's house where I'd offered to take her for a ride in my death mobile a little more than a year ago. I took the ring out of the glove compartment and asked her to marry me. She said yes, but in the next breath sighed and said, "What are we going to do about my parents?"

We decided to do the proper thing and hope for the best. We drove to Coraopolis so that I could ask Anita's father for permission to marry his daughter. He wasn't happy, but, when I told him I was converting to the Catholic Church, he brought out a bottle of Jim Beam and we reluctantly toasted each other. While Anita's father and I sat in the living room and talked about family and religion, Anita spent the evening in the kitchen trying to calm down her hysterical mother, who kept shouting, "How could you be so stupid?"

We spent Christmas Eve at the home of Anita's grandmother, her "Babci," and in the company of her disapproving and suspicious aunts, uncles, and cousins. It was my first serious encounter with Anita's Polish relatives and with Polish food. When Babci placed a heaping platter of pierogis in front of me, Anita leaned over and whispered, "Don't take the ones with the dark center. They're prunes." When I reached for a more innocuous looking pierogi, Anita touched my arm, shook her head, and whispered "sauerkraut." Finally, she guided me to a friendly pile of pierogis filled with cheese and potatoes. When Babci beamed as I loaded up my plate, I knew I had at least one ally in the Homich clan.

We spent Christmas Day with my family, where the food was less adventuresome and the atmosphere more tolerant. My mother wasn't thrilled with our decision to marry after graduation and live near Edinboro, but she liked and respected Anita and went along with our plans. My father thought I was damn lucky that I'd found a "looker" like Anita and enjoyed flirting with her. A year earlier, he'd lost a foot after a bakery truck that he was directing out of a gas station driveway rolled over and crushed it. But, to our amazement, he'd learned to walk with a prosthetic foot and enjoyed taking Anita and me, if I "wanted to come along," around the corner for a few beers. For the first time in my life, thanks to Anita, I felt that I was getting to know my father and we were becoming friends.

When Anita and I returned to Edinboro for our final semester, I began my studies with the local priest for my conversion to Catholicism. Father Dan was a young, liberal-minded priest who seemed more interested in talking about literature than gaining my soul for the Church. We'd spend our winter evenings together listening to Richard Burton recite Shakespeare's soliloquies while sipping Father Dan's rum toddies. In the spring, we put Richard Burton aside, and, like an accommodating Leopold Bloom, I made my conversion, for Anita's sake, to Catholicism.

In the spring Anita and I also applied for teaching positions at elementary and high schools in the Edinboro area. There were plenty of teaching positions available, so we looked around and finally decided to take jobs in the small town of Corry, near Erie, where Anita would teach second grade and I would teach senior English, no more *Bambi* for me, and coach baseball and basketball. We decided to spend one last summer at home earning some money and set our Polish wedding for August.

All that changed when I was selected, as the first of five outstanding seniors from Pennsylvania state colleges, to serve in a new internship program at the Department of Public Instruction in Harrisburg, while earning my Masters degree in education at Bucknell University. To draw attention to the new program, I was invited to Harrisburg for a photo op with the governor. Anita's father knew I'd never make it to Harrisburg in the death mobile, so he lent me his car and trusted me with his daughter for the trip. Anita and I pulled into Harrisburg early in the morning, took a room at the Harrisburger "to freshen up," and emerge a few hours later to meet and shake hands with Governor Scranton. In the photograph, Anita appears to be glowing, while I looked like I'd swallowed a canary.

Once we learned that I had to spend the summer taking graduate courses at Bucknell, Anita and I decided to move our wedding up to July so that we could be together in Lewisburg, a decision that convinced Anita's mother more than ever that her daughter was pregnant. But Anita's father, who had more faith in his daughter, didn't see a problem with Anita or the change in date. He took me to the local Ford dealer where I bought a car, a dark blue Mustang that was a sure bet to make it to Lewisburg and outrace every car and truck on the Pennsylvania turnpike along the way.

On July 17, Anita and I exchanged vows at St. Joseph's in Coraopolis and then survived a rowdy Polish wedding reception filled with drunken relatives on both sides, the odors of kielbasa and pierogis, and the strains of "The Pennsylvania Polka" and "She's Too Fat for Me." We also had the traditional Polish wedding dance, where guests danced with the bride but only after putting money in a basket for the honor. That evening we drove off in our new Mustang and spent the evening at the Hilton in Downtown Pittsburgh, where we sat on

Meeting Governor Scranton, 1965

the bed, sipped champagne from the bottle left on the driver's seat by Anita's boy next door, and counted up the badly needed money from the wedding reception.

The next morning we left Pittsburgh and drove off to Lewisburg and spent a brief honeymoon in our apartment above a five-and-ten, where Anita shopped when I was attending classes. In late August we moved downstate to Harrisburg, where Anita had a new teaching position and I began my internship on my way to a career in state government. It was the first time in my life that Pittsburgh wasn't my home. We'd often visit our families in Pittsburgh, but my home was now with Anita. In college I'd read Thomas Wolfe and James Agee and their lyrical laments that, once you leave, you can't go home again. But I was so caught up in my new life with Anita that I was blind to any loss in leaving home until an emotional shock reminded me of the importance of what I'd left behind.

Chapter 9

In 1995, nearly fifty years after my father took me to Forbes Field for my first major-league game, I finally visited the Baseball Hall of Fame. While in Cooperstown, I asked Tim Wiles, the Director of Research at the National Hall of Fame Library, if he could find the box score of a game played in 1948 between the Pittsburgh Pirates and the Cincinnati Reds. I was convinced it was the first baseball game that I saw with my father.

The problem for those of us who think we remember our first baseball game is that we tend to embellish the truth. If the likes of Mickey Mantle hit a home run every time a kid like comedian Billy Crystal went with his father to his first Yankee game, Mantle's baseball heroics would have rivaled the larger-than-life feats of Pecos Bill, Paul Bunyan, and that steel-bending Pittsburgh folk-hero Joe Magarac. But Mantle struck out far more than he hit home runs, hobbled out to center field on bad legs, ruined his health with drink, and, now and then, lost the big game and broke down in tears, as Pittsburghers found out to our delight in 1960.

The problem with my memory of that buried Pirates-Reds game of 1948, beyond recalling enough details to give Tim Wiles a chance to find the treasured box score, was that what I remembered about the game seemed to out glow Billy Crystal's recollection in emotion and exaggeration. In my mind's eye, the game was played in the spring of 1948, making me nine years old at the time. The Pirates won the game 8–4, and Ralph Kiner, the Mantle of my South Side childhood, hit not one but two home runs off Ewell Blackwell, a tall, lean, side-winding right-hander who had an intimidating reputation for throwing at batters and once said that he knew Kiner was afraid of him. Kiner, after he retired, actually admitted that Blackwell was "a scary pitcher. . . . Your legs shook when you tried to dig in on him because of his sidearm delivery. Yet I hit more home runs off Blackwell than any right-handed batter."

Well, I learned from oral history that Kiner was scared, but he did hit a lot of home runs off Blackwell, the baseball-slinging villain of my youth. And when I opened an envelope from the Baseball Hall of Fame a few weeks after my visit to Cooperstown, I discovered that Kiner had hit two of those home runs off Blackwell in a game played on May 2, 1948, and won by the Pirates 6–4, not 8–4 as I'd remembered it.

When that box score arrived from Cooperstown, I felt as if I'd received a gift from the baseball gods, thanks to mercurial Tim Wiles, a magical summons to go back to the day when my father took me out of the South Side to my first big-league game at Forbes Field. Here were the names of ballplayers to conjure up a perfect memory from my childhood—not only larger-than-life Ralph Kiner but local heroes like Frankie Gustine, who owned a restaurant just up the street from Forbes Field, and Danny Murtaugh, destined to manage the 1960 and 1971 World Championship Pirates.

There was even a delightful surprise waiting for me on the page of box scores copied and sent by Tim Wiles. In the brief summary of the game played the day before, on May 1, 1948, between the Pirates and the Reds, I read that a windmill-winding Pirates pitcher with the wonderful baseball name of Fritz Ostermueller had "hurled the rampaging Pirates into first place, one half game ahead of the Giants." That meant that the Pirates, doomed to be the doormat of the National League through most of my childhood, were in first place on May 2, 1948, though they were to finish fourth that year.

I also discovered in the game summary that Ewell Blackwell had already beaten the Pirates twice in 1948 and had won every game he pitched against them in 1947. But those understanding baseball gods had decreed that Kiner would hit two home runs on May 2, 1948, in his first two times at bat, and the Pirates would finally beat that mean son-of-a-bitch Blackwell and stay in first place—all, of course, because I'd taken the magical journey from the polluted, working-class South Side to palatial and magical Forbes Field for the first time.

With the summary and statistics of the game in front of me, I could now imagine standing with my father at the entrance to the Brady Street Bridge, under the billboard advertising Duquesne Pilsner, the Prince of Beers, as we waited for the 77/54 Bloomfield to turn the corner up at Carson Street and take us out to Forbes Field. I could feel myself jostled about in the overcrowded streetcar (there were over 30,000 fans at the game) as it clattered its way across the bridge, swayed onto Forbes Avenue, passed high above the river and mills until it crossed under the Boulevard of the Allies, only to begin its crawl through Oakland traffic, past the Juvenile Court building, past the Strand with its movie posters for a Gene Autry matinee double bill, until it finally reached Bouquet Street, where I lined up in front of my father and waited impatiently until it was my turn to step down from the streetcar.

In my mind's eye, I can see myself crossing Forbes Street with my father and following the host of fans toward the ballpark as everything around me explodes with sound. Vendors cry out to the crowd to buy miniature bats, autographed baseballs, Pirates pennants, and glossies of Ralph Kiner, Dixie Walker, and Rip Sewell. Others want me to try on a brand-new Pirates cap, just the thing if I'm going to sit in the left-field bleachers, or demand that Pirates fans "get your scorecard here" instead of waiting until we get inside the ballpark. And once we reach Bouquet and Sennot, where the wondrously seductive odor of the grilled "red hots" at Tom and Jerry's floats through the air, I look up for the first time at Forbes Field, at its towering white clay facade, its array of high-arched entrances topped by large awnings, and its green-painted steel girders holding the massive, three-tiered concrete oval in place. And most amazing of all, I hear the sounds of batting practice as I stand with my father at the stately entrance to Forbes Field.

But that's the moment, the very moment when the sounds of baseball beckon me to the pleasure palace of my youth, that my memory takes an odd turn. Rather than paying our way into the ballpark, my father and I cross over to the Home Plate Café. Instead of passing through an underground world of rusted beams and pillars on our way to our general admission seats along the first-base line, we enter the gloomy atmosphere of the Home Plate Café and sit down on bar stools. Instead of emerging from the underbelly of the grandstand, finding our seats, and gazing out at all the green grass and open space, at the giant scoreboard and red-bricked outfield wall, as I listen to my father talk about the fabled history of the ballpark, I sit at the bar and stare at its hanging photographs. There's the clumsy-looking figure of Honus Wagner shaking hands with a youthful Ty Cobb, a smiling Pie Traynor, crouched over, ball and glove in place, waiting to tag out a runner, and the Waner brothers, "Big and Little Poison," sitting one behind the other, bats in hands, as I drink my bottle of Coke and wait anxiously for my father to finish another glass of Iron City before he takes me to the game.

My memory of sitting in the Home Plate Café before my first Pirates game is as vivid to me as sitting in the general-admission seats behind first base during the game, but that box score, the Hall of Fame validation of my perfect childhood memory tells me I'm dead wrong, that I never entered the Home Plate Café on May 2, 1948. The single game I remember so vividly as being played on a glorious, sunny Saturday afternoon was really played as the first game of a doubleheader on a gloomy, rainy Sunday. As for the missing second game, the box score summary claims, "Rain that fell throughout the first contest prevented nightcap." I clearly remember Kiner, Blackwell, but not a drop of rain and certainly not Sunday, because if my cherished game took place on Sunday, then the Home Plate Café had to be closed because of Pennsylvania's Blue Laws. In the baseball Sundays of my South Side childhood, I watched my father drink his Iron City beer and play poker at the private Duquesne Social Club, while I listened to Rosey Rowswell and the Pirates on the radio and, if my father had a run of good luck, played games of shuffleboard bowling.

In *A Death in the Family,* James Agee wrote, "How far we all come. How far we all come away from ourselves. So far, so much in between, you can never go home again. You can go home. It's good to go home, but you never really get all the way home again in your life." Agee believed that having children was the only way of returning to how we felt when we were young, but I also believe that our most important childhood recollections, like the memory of my first game at Forbes Field, though risky and even misleading, also are a way back home for those us who suddenly feel cut off or exiled from our past.

This sense of loss began for me at a time when my thoughts were far removed from the need to get all the way home again. In August 1966, my wife Anita and I had moved to Kent, Ohio, after a frustrating first year

157

living in Harrisburg, Pennsylvania. The internship with the Department of Instruction that promised so much a year ago had turned into a major disappointment. The administrators responsible for the program had no idea of what to do with their new interns, so we often sat around and played brain exercise games instead of working on actual projects. At Bucknell, we were so indoctrinated in our graduate courses with the application of B. F. Skinner's experiments to education that we often felt like rats running through our own maze. At one point our professor proudly presented us with a matrix on classroom behavior that gave points for sound—the more sound, the more active and better the classroom. He was highly displeased when we pointed out that the best model for the classroom, according to his matrix, was a prison riot.

Anita and I became so unhappy with our situation in Harrisburg that I started to apply to graduate schools. When Bob Carothers, my fraternity brother and roommate at Edinboro, contacted us about the graduate program at Kent State University, we decided to make the move. In the middle of July 1966, a year after our wedding, we packed up and left for Kent, Ohio, where, frustrated with bureaucratic games and state bureaucrats, we hoped to become part of the academic life and finally start a family.

A few weeks later and nearly two years after a truck crushed my father's foot in a gas station accident, my mother phoned me at Kent State to let me know that my father was back in the hospital. Her call was different from the one she'd made to Edinboro two years earlier. There was no shock this time, no strained voice telling me my father was probably going to lose his foot. Instead of hearing about the "pins" holding my father's foot together and the threat of gangrene and amputation, I listened to my mother's tired and distressed voice tell me she had to put my father in the hospital because he stopped "cleanin' himself" and finally just wouldn't get out of bed.

A day later, as we drove the few blocks up to the South Side Hospital, my mother told Anita and me what the doctor was telling her. What was "wrong" with my father "was all in his head." The doctor was saying my father was "all depressed over losin' his foot." He was "gonna need treatment," but she wasn't sure what that meant. She just hoped it "wasn't gonna be that shock treatment shit you see in the movies. I just ain't puttin' your dad through that." The doctor even wanted to know if there was any history of mental illness in our family as if "we're all a bunch of loonies." My mother also warned us that my father was so bad he might not say anything or even recognize us.

When we got to the hospital ward, my father did seem to recognize us and did say something when he saw me, though it was only the phrase "apples, peaches, pears, or plums." Those were the last words my father ever said to me. The next morning he slipped into a coma, and he died a few hours later.

While Anita and I sat with my mother in the private room where my father had been moved and where we'd listened to his death rattle, I couldn't explain to my mother why the doctor had said my father wasn't right in his head when "any fool could see he was sick." But I could explain my father's last words. The day before, when he saw me, he must have remembered a game of ball I'd played as a child down on Merriman Way, where each of the players had to take the name of a fruit. The player with the ball would yell out "apples, peaches, pears, or plums," throw the ball high into the air, and call out the fruit of another player. That player, if he caught the ball on the fly, would repeat the ritual; but if the ball hit the ground before he caught it, he'd yell out "freeze," take aim, and try to hit one of the other players with the ball to put him out of the game.

As I listened to my mother's bitter words, I realized that my father, the day before, had probably drifted back to his own playing time as a child and chanted the words of a game we'd both played down on Merriman Way. I could imagine my father hearing again the name of his fruit called out by his brother Tony or Joky and running after the flung ball before it bounced crazily on the alley's red bricks. If he ran fast enough, he could catch the ball on the fly, yell out, "apples, peaches, pears, or plums," before tossing the ball high into the air and calling out the name of Tony's or Joky's fruit. If the ball bounced or was dropped, he had to race down the alley to get safely beyond throwing distance before one of his brothers yelled, "freeze" and tried to put him out of the game.

My father's death was just the beginning of an emotional ordeal for my mother. When she decided to bury my father with his parents in the family plot at St. Casimir's Cemetery, Father Walter, the parish priest, did everything he could to prevent the burial. My father, when he worked at Hoder's gas station, may have taken could care of Father

Walter's Cadillac at no expense to the parish, but that was hardly enough to allow for a special dispensation for a Catholic who hadn't been to confession or communion since he married outside the faith.

When my mother went ahead with the arrangements, despite Father Walter's protest, the priest failed to show up at the Wenslovas funeral home to lead the mourners in an evening prayer at the end of visitations. The next day, though he conducted the required mass, Father Walter refused to deliver any words of comfort to our family. When the mass ended, the funeral director told us that the priest was "feeling too ill" to attend to my father's body at the cemetery. So my mother had to endure one last humiliation before she finally laid my father to rest and moved on with her life. As I watched my mother's bitterness and grief at the cemetery, I prayed that my devout grandmother and wife were right, that there was a Catholic God, and that he would make sure that Father Walter burned in Hell for his terrible cruelty to my family.

After my father's funeral, Anita and I returned to Kent, where, for the next three years, amidst a growing swirl of civil rights and antiwar protests, I completed my graduate degrees and Anita gave birth to our two daughters, Anne and Amy. In 1969, a year before the student killings at Kent, I finished my Ph.D., turned down a teaching position at Edinboro State, though Anita and I badly wanted to go back to our old school and our fondest memories, and accepted, at the urging of my dissertation director, a more prestigious position at Southern Illinois University.

We figured that we'd live in southern Illinois for a few years, and then, after I found a similar position at Pitt, Duquesne, or Carnegie-Mellon, we'd return with our children to our hometown for the rest of our lives. But the academic job market collapsed in the early 1970s and with it our hopes of returning to the Pittsburgh area. What look like a three-year stay in southern Illinois turned into a permanent exile.

During that period, Anita and I, with our growing family of two daughters and our son, Stephen, packed our kids in the car and visited Pittsburgh three or four times a year. We'd first stay in Coraopolis where, after the death of Anita's father, her mother and I worked out an uneasy truce for the sake of her grandchildren. After a few days, we'd drive over to the South Side, where my mother was living in a house bought for her by her boyfriend, Ben, shortly after the death of my father.

American Gothic at Kent State, 1968

Each time I returned to my old neighborhood, it seemed about the same as it was when I was growing up, though both of us were beginning to show signs of age and decay. It wasn't until Pittsburgh's rust-belt depression during the late 1970s and early 1980s that the South Side began a major physical decline. During that period, with more than forty major steel mills and industrial plants closing, Pittsburgh lost 130,000 jobs. An estimated 176,000 people left the area, including 14 percent of its young working force. Even the Pirates threatened to leave the city, until the franchise was rescued from becoming the New Orleans Pirates by a group of Pittsburgh corporations and private investors.

With the loss of Jones and Laughlin and its other steel mills, the South Side became an economic wasteland. Besides its mills, the South

Side also lost most of its other businesses and establishments, including its greasy spoons, movie houses, dairy stores, and gas stations. Only its beer joints continued to thrive during the rust belt depression. I wasn't upset when I drove by and saw Hoder's Gulf station, my post–high school gulag, all boarded up, but losing the Arcade and the Colonial movie houses and my high school hangouts, like Lipori's and George's, was a disturbing reminder that my old neighborhood was fading away and, with it, the road map to the memories of my childhood.

I had no idea, as I watched the deterioration of my old working-class neighborhood, that the South Side, in the last decade of the twentieth century, would begin a remarkable economic and cultural metamorphosis. Today, the South Side, once distinct because of the pungent odor from the Duquesne Brewery and the black soot from Jones and Laughlin, is a yuppyland of trendy art galleries, antique shops, bookstores, and coffee shops. Where steelworkers and Gimbels truck drivers once sat on bar stools at Kalka's and Kotula's, drank their shot-and-a-beer combination and sometimes mixed them into boilermakers, poets now gather at City Books for evening public readings. On weekends, yuppies descend from the suburbs to shoot weekend pool at Shootz Café and Billiards or sit in the art-deco surroundings at the Club Café, once the not-so-proud sponsors of my old Blacksheep softball team, to watch everything from local or touring comedians to rock and folk groups.

Carson Street and environs, once heavily populated by beer joints and greasy spoons, are now dotted with some of Pittsburgh's finest restaurants. If upscale Pittsburghers are looking for the city's best overall restaurant, the reader's poll in the trendy *Pittsburgh Magazine* recommends the Café Allegro, with its "Riviera flair," located down on Twelfth Street in the shadow of the old Market House. If they want to sample the best French menu in Pittsburgh, the poll suggests Le Pommier, "known for its pâté and duck," on Twenty-first and Carson. For a "sunny touch of Spain," all they need to do is go up a block to Twenty-second and Carson to the spot where Bianchini's used to offer a daily luncheon special of a hot Italian sausage sandwich and a draft of Iron City to working-class South Siders of a past generation, including a miserable seventeen-year-old gas station attendant working across the street at Hoder's.

Along the banks of the Monongahela River, where I played hooky in the late 1940s and early 1950s from Humboldt Grade School and South High, my childhood haven of overgrown weeds and half-buried debris is gone, replaced by River Front Park with its public benches, picnic tables, and boat docks. Even the ball fields of my youth at Ormsby and Armstrong playgrounds and the football field at South High, now renamed Cupples Stadium, have undergone a strange and wondrous change. On all-dirt playground fields so dry and dusty in the hot summer months that city workers had to oil them, grass now reluctantly grows in the outfield. And on my old rock-hard football field, the memories of lopsided games lost to Westinghouse, Peabody, and Allderdice are buried under a layer of bouncy artificial turf.

The sight of the new South Side, with its thriving businesses, acclaimed restaurants, and vibrant culture is impressive, but it's the old South Side, with its ethnic enclaves, dusty ball fields, and working-class attitudes that shaped my character and my way of looking at the world. I've spent a good part of my adult life in an academic world that thrives on revised histories and reshaped cultures, but, after my father's death, I'd found it harder and harder to let go of the South Side, no matter what my academic training told me about the seductive and deceptive nature of memory and history. In my mind's eye, the old South Side, even as it receded from social and cultural relevance, is still the home of my unfit schoolmates, my misfit ball-playing buddies, and my mismatched parents.

But the problem, beyond the physical changes, in living away from the South Side for so long is the lost contact with my own generation of South Siders. Every trip back to Pittsburgh, I look for the companions of my youth, but, except for the small gatherings of old-timers on street corner benches or at the back tables in coffee shops, what I find are the unfamiliar, indifferent faces of a new generation. The dialects, the foreign accents, and odd pronunciations of the voices from my childhood are mostly gone. The fragments of passing conversations seem so remote that I sometimes feel as if, in trying to come home again, I've wandered into some undiscovered country.

It's one thing to grow old, to lose our youth to the flowing waters of Heraclitus's river, but it's another thing to lose the reminders of that youth, to have our personal histories erased by physical and generational change. In *A Portrait of the Artist as a Young Man,* Stephen Dedalus, the autobiographical creation of self-exiled James Joyce, declares that "history is a nightmare from which I'm trying to awake," but a worse nightmare is to return to the landscape of our history and find it gone. Norman Mailer once wrote, "To return to an old neighborhood and discover that it has disappeared is a minor woe for some but it is close to a physical catastrophe for others, an amputation."

Having grown up in a narrow, working-class enclave within a large industrial city, most of my childhood memories are of small things—clean base hits and running catches, black-and-white B movies and cliffhangers, cloistered riverbanks and darkened loading docks, greasy spoons and beer joints, odd-shaped playgrounds and inclines, and bad Pirates and Steelers teams. Added up, they hardly seem the stuff of life's great tragedies or comedies. But, while I was growing up, the fathers of my old South Side quietly played out their own small tragedies in mills, warehouses, and gas stations, then drank their lives away on bar stools— while the mothers, without notice, forged their own personal triumphs by keeping their families together and enduring the hard life.

During one of my visits to the South Side, my wife and I went shopping at the local Giant Eagle for a few last-minute groceries we needed for a family gathering to celebrate my mother's eighty-fifth birthday. While we waited in line, there was an altercation at the checkout counter over a container of fruit-flavored yogurt. A white, thirty-something male, well-dressed and well-groomed, angrily complained he was being overcharged. When the checkout clerk tried to explained to the customer that he'd picked up the brand of fruit-flavored yogurt that wasn't on sale by mistake, he told her that he was new to the South Side, was accustomed to "more respect and better service," and ought to ring her "goddam neck" for embarrassing him. Before the store manager could make it up to the counter, the offended, well-heeled customer stormed out of the store, got into his BMW, and was heading for the sanctuary of his riverside town house.

A few hours later, we were on the open-air patio of a South Side convalescent center, where my mother, her frail body severely bent by osteoporosis and racked with arthritis, sat in a wheel chair and listened to three generations of her family sing "Happy Birthday." During the past few months, she'd suffered through the pain of a pathological fracture of her leg, spent time at South Side Hospital in intensive care and a step-down unit after complications from surgery, and nearly died from severe weight loss and malnutrition until a feeding tube was inserted into her stomach. When we finished singing, my mother, instead of weeping or cursing her failing body, took off the straw hat she was wearing to protect her from the sun, and, with a touch of the regal, bowed to her family. Then she rose from the wheelchair and, with the help of a walker, took a few steps just to show us that she was determined to go home.

My mother, despite her determination, was never well enough to leave the convalescent center. She died a little more than a year later after she slipped into a coma and was rushed to South Side Hospital where my father had died over thirty-five years ago. Her death ended a covenant between mother and son that had lasted over forty years.

When I left the South Side in the early 1960s for college, I promised my mother that after graduation I would return to live in Pittsburgh. It was the one thing she wanted in a life of doing without and the one thing I wanted to give her. As the years flowed by, that unfulfilled promise, rather than growing weaker, became our emotional bound. She believed with an absolute faith that I would eventually come home no matter how long I was away. And I kept up my hopeless hope that, despite a collapsed job market in my profession, the perfect college teaching job would materialize at Pitt, Duquesne, or Carnegie Mellon, all the while believing that my mother would live on until I finally kept my promise and came back to Pittsburgh.

Since my mother's death, friends and family have asked me if I still feel the need to return to Pittsburgh. My answer is that Pittsburgh is still my home, but I know that emotionally things aren't the same as before. For years, I watched my mother stand in her doorway and wave good-bye as I drove away after each visit, but that image, once the emotional core of my love for Pittsburgh and the South Side, has now also become a part of a ghostly past. It was as if my mother's life on the South Side had kept the memories of my youth and the community alive and vivid, no matter how long I stayed away or how much the South Side itself changed. With her gone, the old South Side now seemed more and more a community of phantoms, and, for the first time in my life, I felt homeless after so many years of feeling homesick.

The death of my mother all but severed my emotional tie with the South Side, but another loss, which should have been the final cut, brought everything I valued about the old life back to me. Pittsburgh's Board of Public Education, after threatening to close South High in the 1980s, finally decided in the spring of 2004, that, as part of its long-term retrenchment plan, it was time to close my old alma mater, which, over the years, had become Pittsburgh's oldest operating high school.

That summer, after paying my respects to South High with one last visit, I wrote an op-ed piece in the *Pittsburgh Post-Gazette* about the school's closing. In the piece I tried to blend the long history of the school, which dated back to its opening in 1898, with my own reminiscences from the 1950s, sharpened now by what I had seen when I walked through the halls and classrooms for the last time. I also wanted to write something that was a celebration of those who were part of the school's history, rather than a criticism of those responsible for its closing.

It was easy to write the essay. I began with the ceremonial act taken on the final day of classes, when the entire student body departed under the plaque honoring South High's original classroom building as a historical landmark. I added that in a few days, when the current principal locked the doors of South High for good, she would effectively end 106 years of public education at a school that graduated nearly 15,000 students in its service to the community, including my own Cold War generation of students, and became a melting pot for the South Side's ethnic enclaves.

The heart of the essay described my last walk through South High. While so much seemed run-down, there were still vestiges in the original building of its old beauty, like the wrought-iron staircase leading up to the third floor, where South High's first marching band, safely distanced from the student body, blared out its musical scales and tunes. In the basement of the high school's annex, the swimming pool, looking as pristine as it did decades ago, was still filled with water, and the chalkboard menu still announced the last daily special in the same cafeteria where my 1956 graduating class, eating lunch on Senior Day, rose at the sound of fire alarm, sang the school's alma mater, then sat down and finished the scoops of mashed potatoes and stuffing that had sustained us since the seventh grade.

In closing, I wrote that one of the hottest items for sale at this year's South Side Street Spectacular was a blast from the past—an orange and black T-shirt with "South High Orioles 1898–2004" printed on the front and the South High alma mater on the back. I mentioned that if you knew the alma mater and were willing to sing the opening stanza, you got a dollar off on the price of the T-shirt. I also confessed that, to my wife's embarrassment, I sang the entire alma mater before buying the T-shirt.

After the South High essay was published in the *Post-Gazette,* I'd hoped to hear from a South High alumnus or two, but what I received was a flood of e-mails that brought the old South Side back to life for me. My long years of exile and the loss of my parents had finally convinced me that my old neighborhood had become nothing more than a world of shadows and ghosts, but suddenly there was a chorus of voices from Pittsburgh and around the country telling me I wasn't alone and my old neighborhood wasn't forgotten.

Those still living in Pittsburgh wanted me to know of the passing of sadly missed South High classmates and family members. Others, living in retirement in Arizona and Florida, wrote that they were often in touch with old classmates and family still living in Pittsburgh who kept them up to date about life on the South Side. I heard from lawyers, engineers, and educators who credited South High for their success, as well as firemen, policeman, and secretaries, who claimed that the years at South High were the best years of their lives.

The daughter of Mary Jane Schmalstieg, a South Side historian and activist who fought for years against the closing of South High, wrote about the incredible turnout at her mother's funeral and how many friends her mother had, "from the yuppies, to politicians, to the long-time 'everyday' South Side folk." A 1952 graduate wanted me to know she'd reunited with "an old high school boyfriend" at her fiftieth high school reunion and they were now married and living happily in Arizona. I even heard from Beverly Mangan, the vendor who sold the commemorative South High T-shirts at the South Side Street Spectacular. She wrote to let me know that anyone wanting a T-shirt should contact "Moose" at the South Side Beer distributor.

All of the e-mails were wonderful in their warmth and pride, but my favorites came from a few of my old ball-playing buddies. "Cush" Zabinski, who was a teammate at South High, wanted me to know that he and his brother Walt had professional tryouts after graduating and eventually went on to play baseball at major colleges. I also heard from "Chick" Devine, from my softball days at Ormsby, who wanted to know "if the name South Side Black Sheep" meant something to me, and "Buzzy" Karwoski, who often thought of "our old days in the South Side, the Black Sheep and all our old buddies." While I may have lost touch with my "old buddies," there they were, living their lives, keeping in touch with each other, and remembering our old ball-playing days with great affection.

While visions of reunions with my old teammates danced in my head, I also received a reminder of the hard life in Pittsburgh for minorities and the value of sports in uplifting the spirit of those most vulnerable to defeat and despair. George Moses wrote a wonderful e-mail about his love for South High and its community and how he wished he could have taken that last walk through South High's hallways with me and sat down one more time in the school's cafeteria. But he also wanted to know if I remembered "a few of the black kids that left their mark at South. Some of the trophies that were in that small case on the second floor: they helped put there. We are a part of that huge melting pot on the South Side."

I also received a strong reminder of the Pirates ballplayer who had come to epitomize, in my mind, the best and the worst of growing up in Pittsburgh. Beverly Mangan, after telling me about "Moose" and the T-shirts, also wanted to know about the extraordinary thing that happened to her husband "Sluggo" in 1963 at a Pirates game honoring Little League players. During the game, Roberto Clemente cracked his bat, hitting a foul ball: "While walking back from home plate, he handed up the cracked bat to my husband in the stands. . . . A big league ballplayer. . . . the Roberto Clemente." Beverly said that her husband still has Clemente's bat, which he shows to disbelieving friends after telling his story, and that their son was born on August 18, 1973: "Isn't Roberto's birthday the same day in August?"

Beverly Mangan was right about Roberto Clemente's birthday, but the most remarkable thing about her story of Clemente's bat and the coincidence of her son's birthday was the way the two events framed Clemente's career and illuminated his character. When he handed the bat to Beverly's husband, Clemente was on his way to Hall of Fame greatness, but when her son was born, it was on Clemente's first birthday after his death in a tragic plane crash. In 1963, Clemente was a proud, driven ballplayer who felt betrayed by Pittsburgh sportswriters and alienated from the city's fans, but, ten years later, in 1973, his tragic death had transformed him into a Pittsburgh sports legend, worshipped and beloved by sportswriters and fans.

For those of us who grew up with Clemente, there is no better illustration of loyalty to heritage, pride in hard work, and respect for community. Recognized and honored today as "The Great One," Clemente struggled for years in a city badly divided by class and race, but his brilliant career and his tragic sacrifice transformed him into a unifying symbol of nobility and courage. His humanity taught us that, no matter what the circumstances of our lives—no matter the enclave, race, or class—it's possible to find the best part of ourselves in our pride in home and family and in memories as grand as a World Series victory that draws a community together or as small as a broken bat that connects a small boy with a baseball immortal.

On a recent visit to Pittsburgh, Anita and I were driving into the city on a summer Saturday night just as the sky above PNC Park exploded with fireworks. I remember the disbelieving look on Anita's face when I told her that I was glad Pittsburgh was finally going out of its way to welcome me home. As we drove along the river, we passed Station Square and its trendy shops and headed into a swarm of traffic and young people attracted by the South Side's thriving nightlife. When we reached 23rd Street, instead of turning toward my mother's old house, we headed over the Birmingham Bridge to our lodging in Oakland, not too far from the site of old Forbes Field.

For years, we'd driven to Pittsburgh with our children and stayed with my mother at her house on 23rd Street. During our visits, we'd take our kids out to Kennywood Park to ride the roller coasters, to the Carnegie Museum to marvel at the dinosaur bones, and to Three Rivers to make sure they grew up Pirates and Steelers fans. Now that my mother is gone, it's heartbreaking to bypass her house and drive out of the South Side and over the Birmingham Bridge, but I have a feeling that if I looked down, over the railing, I'd see my mother standing in the doorway, still patiently waiting for me and faithful to the South Side of my childhood.

Acknowledgments

There have been many storytellers who contributed to the narrative of *Growing Up With Clemente.* They range from my old classmates to my old ball-playing buddies. Their memories of the classrooms and ball fields of my youth were often sharper than my own recollections. I talked with so many family members and old friends it's simply impossible to mention all their names, but I'd like to recognize the late Mary Jane Schmalsteig, a local historian, for providing me with so much material on the old South Side that, at times, it seemed as if she had given me a road map to the past.

I would like to thank Randy Roberts, Lee Gutkind, and David Shribman for giving me my first opportunities to write about Pittsburgh and John Allison and Greg Victor for their support and advice. I'm also grateful to Laurie Graham for her willingness to read my work in progress and her valuable suggestions for sharpening my memories and vision of Pittsburgh. And I need to thank Mike Magnuson for his advice on the practical challenges of writing creative nonfiction.

I owe my greatest debt to Eileen Glass for her skill and patience in preparing the manuscript. It was her good cheer and friendship that often made the difference between going on or giving up. The book would never have been completed without her dedication. I would also like to give my special thanks to Joanna Hildebrand Craig for giving the manuscript a clear sense of direction and form and to Mary Young for shepherding the manuscript through its revisions.

In closing, I would like to give my loving gratitude to my wife, Anita, for so many wonderful gifts over the years, none greater than our three children, Anne, Amy, and Stephen. Since our first days together in college, when we created our own little world, she has been my best friend and constant companion. Our years together have been my greatest blessing and the best years of my life.

Portions of the book in different formats previously appeared in the *Pittsburgh Post-Gazette, Pittsburgh Sports: Stories from the Steel City, Lessons in Persuasion: Creative Nonfiction/Pittsburgh Connections,* and the *Crab Orchard Review.*